In this compelling book, I
looked and often misunde

A friend of mine often says that we are seeing in the modern church "a culture of celebrity," and this culture has in many ways moved all the action from the pew to the pulpit, from the seats to the stage, from the people to the preachers. In this book, Dr. Earley reminds us of what Paul says in Ephesians: that spiritual gifts are given for the perfecting of the saints so that they can do the work of ministry. Teaching people that they have a calling, helping them find their gift(s), and then making room in the Body for them is not just the job of the church but the joy of the church.

Read this book and be challenged—read this book and be changed.

Bishop Timothy J. Clarke
Columbus, Ohio

Dr. Kevin W. Earley calls the church of the twenty-first century to move beyond the rhetoric of the priesthood of all believers to the reality of all members of the body of Christ doing ministry based on spiritual gifts. *Every-Member Ministry* establishes a theological basis for a liberated ministry and then gives practical steps to equip women and men for effective service. I recommend this book for all leaders who desire to see the church empowered to teach, fellowship, and serve.

David A. Sebastian, Dean
Anderson University
School of Theology

The priesthood of all believers is something we affirm and teach but often have difficulty fully implementing in our churches. Kevin W. Earley provides individual readers and study groups an opportunity to explore the biblical teaching of spiritual gifts and practically relate it to their congregation's ministries. This is a much needed discussion today, and *Every Member Ministry* will surely assist in bringing this to the forefront and mobilizing the entire church.

Lloyd Moritz, Executive Director
Pacific Northwest Association of the Church
of God

EVERY-MEMBER

Spiritual Gifts and God's
Design for Service

Kevin W. Earley

Anderson, Indiana

Published by Warner Press Inc.
Warner Press and the "WP" logo are trademarks of Warner Press Inc.

Warner Press Inc.
PO Box 2499
Anderson, IN 46018-2499
800-741-7721
www.warnerpress.org

ISBN (pbk): 978-1-59317-644-0
ISBN (ePub): 978-1-59317-645-7
ISBN (Kindle): 978-1-59317-646-4

Library of Congress Cataloging-in-Publication Data

Earley, Kevin W.
Every-member ministry : spiritual gifts and God's design for service / Kevin W. Earley.
    pages   cm
Includes bibliographical references and index.
ISBN 978-1-59317-644-0 (pbk. : alk. paper) -- ISBN 978-1-59317-645-7 (epub : alk. paper) -- ISBN 978-1-59317-646-4 1. Gifts, Spiritual. I. Title.
BT767.3.E25 2013
234'.13--dc23   2013031238

Printed in the United States of America.

Contents

Part One: Foundational Principles

Part Two: Building Upon the Foundation

Part Three: Surveying Specific Spiritual Gifts

Acknowledgements

I would like to thank Dr. David Markle, Dr. John Aukerman, and Dr. James Earl Massey for the invaluable direction they provided when I originally wrote this work as a lecture series within my dissertation/project for the doctor of ministry degree. I thank Dr. Robert O. Dulin Jr., who preceded me as the senior pastor of Metropolitan Church of God, for his unwavering support of my service to the Lord. I would also like to thank the Metropolitan Church of God family, for they have encouraged and supported me throughout my pastoral journey thus far. I would like to convey my gratitude to Dr. E. Raymond Chin, who pastored and mentored me through my metamorphosis from lay minister to full-time pastor. I express my deepest gratitude to the memory of my mother, Rita Joyce Williams. She ushered me into a personal relationship with Jesus Christ, taught me how to hold onto God's unchanging hand, and allowed her life to preach to me each day during the twenty-eight years we were blessed to live on earth at the same time. Although her eyes never read the lines of this book, her influence extends to each and every page. I extend my love and appreciation to my Babe, Precious Ann Earley; she is the love of my life, partner in ministry, and mother of our three children. My love also extends to Kevin Wesley Jr., Kaleb Van, and Ky Elise, the greatest toddlers in the world. Finally, I pray this book brings pleasure to Jesus Christ, my Lord and Savior.

Foreword

Those who pastor have the sacred task of helping individuals deal with their personal needs, problems, and possibilities in the light of Christian faith and in the setting of congregational life. That task is both spiritual and specialized in nature, and it requires not only a divine call but a distinct conditioning and commitment to serve people.

This book, written by a pastor, is designed to assist others in locating their place of service in the church and in the world as a representative of Christ. The theme basis is "every-member ministry," and each chapter sets forth insights to equip and motivate the reader to be engaged in some specific service as a believer.

Mindful that many in our time are uninformed or misinformed about how ministry is understood, valued, and demonstrated in Scripture, Dr. Earley has deftly traced this in the Old Testament narratives as well as the New Testament. His foundational concern has been to prod the reader to become distinctly active, serving in his or her God-gifted role without feeling inferior, envious, or independent.

This book by Dr. Earley is a timely gift to the universal church. It is an excellent and needed teaching tool from a pastor concerned to foster the development of members who know and use their gifts instinctively to God's glory in both the church and the world.

James Earl Massey
Dean Emeritus and Distinguished
Professor at Large
Anderson University School of Theology

Introduction

Throughout the history of Christianity, the people of God have had priests, prophets, pastors, evangelists, and other forms of clergy to lead the way. God continues to call women and men to full-time ministry; however, not every believer is called to ordained ministry. Not all Christians are commissioned to stand behind a sacred desk and preach the word, serve Communion, get up in the middle of the night to take care of church emergencies, solemnize marriages, or perform funerals.

While God has not called every believer *to* the ministry, He has called all believers *to do* ministry. It is important that every child of God grasp the fact that, like Moses, Isaiah, the twelve disciples, and a host of others, we are called to serve the Lord and other people to the glory of God. All Christians are empowered by God in some way to be servants, catalysts for change, and agitators for transformation. To this end, the Holy Spirit graces every Christian with at least one spiritual gift. In other words, every believer possess a piece of the larger puzzle called ministry. Therefore, the every-member ministry of a local congregation is God's design for service and his method for establishing his will on earth as it is in heaven.

However, Christian congregations often have a small group of church members sustaining the majority of their ministries. The evidence of this arises when church members express one or more of the following opinions that hinder an all-inclusive approach to ministry involvement:

- The pastoral staff has the primary responsibility to do ministry.

- The role of the pastor is to serve the members of the congregation.

- The pastoral staff ministers on behalf of the congregation.

- When one identifies a need in the congregation or community, it should be brought to the pastor's attention so that he or she can address it.

- The benchmark of faithful church membership is attendance at services and programs.

- Life as a Christian centers on meeting one's own spiritual and physical needs.

- A congregation's use of spiritual gifting is important, but not practical.

- Church members are misguided if they expect other Christians to identify and offer their spiritual gifting to the congregation.

- Ministry involvement must be initiated by pastoral appointment.[1]

This book rejects such notions. It is designed to enable and motivate an all-inclusive ministry in which all members of a congregation minister. It also aims to inject the expectation of ministry participation into the ethos of congregations.

In Part 1, the foundational principles of an every-member ministry are outlined. We consider the biblical principle that every Christian is called to ministry and functions as a priest or minister in the local congregation. The scriptural criteria for a disciple's true greatness are highlighted. Finally, we define what spiritual gifts are and consider how to identify them in an individual's life before we unpack the gift discovery process. This is why we discuss the gift discovery process at the end

---

1. *Ministry involvement* is defined as that which occurs when parishioners engage in the service the local congregation renders to those within and outside of the church. Ministry involvement is also characterized by parishioners who function in their priestly roles by using their spiritual gifts to edify others.

of Part 1; you are strongly encouraged to absorb the biblical principles described in chapters 1–3 prior to beginning the gift discovery process.

Part 2 further raises our level of awareness of God's design for Christian service. Here we explore the implications of Christ's supreme leadership, along with the local church's responsibility to serve those outside its walls through evangelism and social action. We cite several dangers that can disrupt God's design for service. We examine an important Old Testament text that teaches us that God has always empowered the community of believers to accomplish work on his behalf instead of relying on a sole minister. Lastly, we consider several specific methods for engaging in Christian social action.

What are some of the gifts of the Spirit? In what ways does the Spirit equip believers so they can effectively minister? Part 3 endeavors to provide answers to these questions. Chapter 9 scrutinizes the spiritual gifts described in 1 Corinthians 12, which contains the longest list of spiritual gifts in the Bible. Chapters 10–12 organize spiritual gifts by categories. Based on the definition in chapter 3 of a spiritual gift, the absence of an exhaustive list of spiritual gifts in Scripture, and my conviction that the Holy Spirit may continue to create spiritual gifts as he deems necessary now and in the future, I have chosen to call some kinds of unusual spiritual enablement for ministry *spiritual gifts* although they are not specifically listed in the Bible.[2] Others may prefer to call these *spiritual empowerments*. However one classifies each manifestation of the Holy Spirit's work, it is important to understand that the Holy Spirit graces the church with a variety of tools so that every member of the church can minister.

Each chapter has objectives, a lesson, and a quiz. One group of Christian educators defines *objectives* as "hoped-for outcomes of the [lesson], stated in terms of what the students will do in the [lesson]. There are usually three objectives for each lesson (one cognitive, one affective, and one behavioral), because learning is not complete until we KNOW something, FEEL something, and DO something."[3] The

---

2. The absence of a biblical reference will serve as an indicator in chapters ten, eleven, and twelve that a specific manifestation meets the criteria of being a spiritual gift but is not specifically listed in Scripture.

3. Aukerman, Smythe, and Starr, *Christian Relationships*, iv.

lesson is the biblical information to be grasped, and we have attempted to present each lesson in a variety of ways while citing a host of resources for further study along the way. The *quiz* may take the form of a pre-lesson or post-lesson questionnaire, intended to reemphasize important concepts of each week's study.

As you prepare to take this journey through every-member ministry, I invite you to consider the caterpillar. The caterpillar has many legs and crawls on the ground. It tends to have bad vision and a soft, vulnerable body. In fact, the only thing hard about a caterpillar is its head! A lot of other creatures like to feed on caterpillars, and their primary defense is to imitate the world around them. Farmers consider them pests because they devour so much food. They eat and eat and eat, giving nothing valuable in return.

One day the caterpillar enters a cocoon, where it experiences a great transformation, a metamorphosis. As a result, the caterpillar becomes a butterfly! It no longer crawls on the ground or has limited vision, so it is no longer as vulnerable as it had been. After its metamorphosis, it soars to heights it would have never reached as a caterpillar, pollinating flowers as it goes.

I pray that this book will cause a metamorphosis in your life, so that you do not simply devour spiritual resources but soar to new heights as you are spiritually equipped to serve in ways that honor Jesus Christ.

CHAPTER 1

Priesthood of All Believers

Objectives

1. Discover that God calls all Christians to serve as priests and ministers in the church.
2. Cherish our ability to serve in our local congregation.
3. Commit ourselves to serving in our congregation's ministries.

The following words, written by Dr. Carter G. Woodson in 1933, have agitated thought for decades: "When you control a man's thinking you do not have to worry about his actions. You do not have to tell him not to stand here or go yonder. He will find his 'proper place' and will stay in it. You do not need to send him to the back door. He will go without being told. In fact, if there is no back door, he will cut one for his special benefit. His education makes it necessary."[1]

Although Woodson was referring to a different context, his comment is relevant for the body of Christ today. Satan, our spiritual Enemy, would love to control the way we think so that we are unaware of our calling as priests in the kingdom. If we are uninformed or ill-informed about the ministry God has given us, the body of Christ

---

1. Woodson, *Mis-Education of the Negro*, xiii.

will have a mediocre impact on the world. Therefore, the church must reject every notion that would keep us from functioning as the Spirit intends.

Specifically, the church must reject the faulty notions that (1) ministry belongs to the clergy community alone, (2) clergypersons are supposed to minister on behalf of or in the place of the other members of a local congregation, and (3) the benchmark of faithful Christian discipleship hinges on regular worship attendance alone. W. Franklin Richardson states, "In most of our churches, we suffer from a perspective that hinders the church from realizing the empowerment that the pew possesses. A prevailing mentality exists in many of our pews that the responsibility for ministry rests with the clergy or the ordained community the congregation hires to do its ministry. This mentality keeps the laity from realizing its potential to do ministry."[2]

Scripture emphasizes the truth that authentic biblical ministry is the province of all the people of God. Exodus 18:13–27 stands as a clear example. This text describes how Moses attempted to serve as the judge for all of the Israelite people, settling the disputes they had between each other. This became a bureaucratic nightmare. The people stood around night and day, waiting to have their cases heard by Moses. Jethro, Moses's father-in-law, advised Moses to focus on representing the people before God by selecting and training capable men to help shoulder the burden of everyday civil disputes. Under the proposed new structure, Moses would continue to judge the difficult cases, but all others would be handled by the officials Moses selected and trained. Jethro's advice revealed God's will for the community. As a result of implementing the new structure, the responsibility to serve was shared and the bureaucratic nightmare was over.

Similarly, the pastors of churches with clergy-centered ministries are prone to ineffectiveness. Kevin Ruffcorn writes, "[Clergy-centered] ministry is, in part, responsible for the declining worship attendance and apathy among members in the majority of mainline denominations. At the same time that clergy-centered ministry has hamstrung

---

2. Richardson, *Power in the Pew*, 9.

the mission of the Church, clergy have experienced increased burnout and depression as they have attempted to do everything." [3]

The body of Christ is tempted to restrict the work of priestly ministry to a group of ordained clergypersons to the exclusion of the laity. Greg Ogden, however, insightfully defines a priest as "a vehicle in whom God lives and through whom God works to bring His presence to others."[4] From a New Testament perspective, the priesthood consists of all Christ's followers, each having been commissioned to represent Christ in the world and to provide access to the Father through Christ. Second Corinthians 5:17–20 sheds light on the subject:

> Therefore, if anyone is in Christ, he is a new creation; the old has gone, the new has come! All this is from God, who reconciled us to himself through Christ *and gave us the ministry of reconciliation*: that God was reconciling the world to himself in Christ, not counting men's sins against them. And he has committed to us the message of reconciliation. We are therefore Christ's ambassadors, as though God were making his appeal through us. We implore you on Christ's behalf: Be reconciled to God. (italics added)

Hebrews 10:19–22 contributes to the discussion as well:

> Therefore, brothers, since *we have confidence to enter the Most Holy Place by the blood of Jesus,* by a new and living way opened for us through the curtain, that is, his body, and since we have a great priest over the house of God, let us draw near to God with a sincere heart in full assurance of faith, having our hearts sprinkled to cleanse us from a guilty conscience and having our bodies washed with pure water. (italics added)

---

3. Ruffcorn, "Recovering the Priesthood of All Believers," 18.

4. Ogden, *Unfinished Business*, 28.

In his book *The Other Six Days,* R. Paul Stevens supplies a helpful argument for the priesthood of all believers as it relates to the Greek word *kleros,* translated as "clergy":

> The term originally means "lot," "share", or "portion assigned to someone," and was used in the Old Testament for the inheritance in the promised land. This term gets transferred to the New Testament from the Greek translation of the Old Testament. Peter and John use this word when they tell Simon Magus he has "no part or share [*kleros*] in this ministry, because your heart is not right before God" (Acts 8:21; cf. Deut. 12:12). But here is the new thing. The Old Testament "inheritance" is now shared with all believers. Jesus says to Saul/Paul, "I am sending you to [the Gentiles] to open their eyes and turn them from darkness to light, and from the power of satan to God, so that they may receive forgiveness of sins and a *place* [*kleron*] among those who are sanctified by faith in me" (emphasis [Steven's], Acts 26:17–18; cf. Eph.1:11; Gal. 3:29; Col. 1:12)." [5]

As a consequence, "lay persons must accept the fact that they have been called of God for some special work that only they can perform."[6] When we accept this fact, we will cease to place ourselves in insignificant roles in the life of the church, though we may be accustomed to them. We will no longer enter the doors of inactivity. In the words of Martin Luther, "Let everyone who knows himself to be a Christian be assured of this, and apply it to himself—we are all priests."[7]

Instead of a singular priest or a small group of priests, "God has chosen to make the body of Christ an *organism,* Jesus being the head and each member functioning with one or more spiritual gifts. Understanding spiritual gifts becomes the foundational key to understanding the organization of the Church."[8]

---

5. Stevens, *Other Six Days,* 31.

6. Phelps, "Motivation and Empowerment of the Laity," 31.

7. Luther, *Works of Martin Luther,* 282.

8. Wagner, *Your Spiritual Gifts,* 29.

Priesthood of All Believers

QUIZ 1
Gifts of the Spirit

Next to each statement write *T* for true or *F* for false.

_____ 1. Only ordained clergy persons perform real ministry in the kingdom of God.

_____ 2. Pastors, priests, and ministers are called to serve in place of the members of the body of Christ who work in secular occupations throughout the week.

_____ 3. Hallmarks of faithful Christian discipleship include having an authentic personal relationship with God, spending time with other Christians, and serving others in the community of faith.

_____ 4. A church that encourages the active participation of all its members is prone to chaos and ineffectiveness.

_____ 5. Every disciple of Christ is a priest—i.e., an active intercessor between needy human beings and a compassionate God.

_____ 6. When a person becomes a Christian, she/he simultaneously becomes a minister.

_____ 7. Showing up for church events is an acceptable substitute for personally serving others in Christ's name.

_____ 8. Growing congregations tend to have clergy-centered ministries.

_____ 9. One of the privileges of being a Christian is sharing in his kingdom work.

_____ 10. My service/involvement in the ministry of my church is just as necessary as the involvement of others.

Further Reflection:

Assess your current involvement in the life of the church. Are you serving as actively as you should be?

CHAPTER 2

Spiritual Gifts According to 1 Corinthians 12

Objectives

1. Explore the practical implications of 1 Corinthians 12:1–11.
2. Learn why identifying and using our spiritual gifts are essential to our Christian discipleship.
3. Determine to offer our own spiritual gifts to strengthen and serve the church.

D r. Martin Luther King Jr. delivered a speech titled "The Drum Major Instinct" to the Ebenezer Baptist Church in Atlanta, Georgia, on February 4, 1968. In it, he stated:

Jesus gave us a new norm of greatness. If you want to be important—wonderful. If you want to be recognized—wonderful. If you want to be great—wonderful. But recognize that he who is great among you shall be your servant. That's a new definition of greatness. And this morning, the thing that I like about it is: by giving that definition of greatness, it means that everybody can be great, because everyone can serve. You don't have to have a college degree to serve. You don't have to make your subject and your verb agree to serve. You don't have to know about Plato and Aristotle to serve. You don't have to know Einstein's theory of relativity to serve. You don't have to know the second theory of thermodynamics in physics to serve. You only need a heart full of grace, a soul generated by love. And you can be a servant.

The apostle Paul probably would have agreed with these words. In fact, long before Martin Luther King Jr. delivered this speech, Paul declared his conviction that every Christian has been graced by the Spirit with a spiritual gift. First Corinthians 12:1-11 serves as a prime example:

Now about spiritual gifts, brothers, I do not want you to be ignorant. You know that when you were pagans, somehow or other you were influenced and led astray to mute idols. Therefore I tell you that no one who is speaking by the Spirit of God says, "Jesus be cursed," and no one can say, "Jesus is Lord," except by the Holy Spirit.

There are different kinds of gifts, but the same Spirit. There are different kinds of service, but the same Lord. There are different kinds of working, but the same God works all of them in all men.

Now to each one the manifestation of the Spirit is given for the common good. To one there is given through the Spirit the message of wisdom, to another the message of knowledge by means of the same Spirit, to another faith by the same Spirit, to another gifts of healing by that one Spirit, to another miraculous powers, to another prophecy, to another distinguishing between spirits, to another speaking in different kinds of tongues, and to still another the interpretation of tongues. All these are the work of one and the same Spirit, and he gives them to each one, just as he determines.

This text clearly teaches that every believer has been graced by the Spirit with a spiritual gift. I prefer to use the phrase "graced with a spiritual gift" over "given a spiritual gift" because these gifts are not distributed for personal use and God has been gracious is allowing believers to possess these gifts so that we can minister to others. Put another way, the spiritual gifts that the Holy Spirit distributes are ultimately intended to benefit the church. It is as if a believer receives a gift box labeled,

TO: The Church
FROM: The Holy Spirit

Randal Huber writes, "Every member of the body, whether male or female, has a God-given role in the church. God wants his body to be an authentic community of men and women, young and old, people from all nations, races, and social classes. Each one is to exercise his or her gifts for the common good."[1] Because every believer has a spiritual gift, every believer has a ministry. Since every believer has a ministry, theoretically and practically, every believer is a minister. One need not be an ordained minister in order to consider oneself a minister appointed by God.

The presence of a believer's spiritual gift stands as a reminder of the Spirit's care and concern for the entire church. A spiritual gift evidences the fact that the Spirit has diagnosed a need in the community of faith and sought to address that need with a spiritual gift he placed in a specific believer. A believer who identifies his or her gift simultaneously identifies the specific way the Spirit intends for them to be a blessing to other Christians. This implies that the Lord not only provides spiritual gifts to individuals but also graciously gifts congregations with persons who possess specific gifts. Therefore, we ought to feel excited when new members begin worshiping and serving in our local congregation.

The Spirit ultimately initiates a Christian's involvement in ministry. Once we correctly identify our spiritual gifting, we should not wait for a pastoral or committee appointment before we ask to be

---

1. Huber, "Advancing the Placement of Women," 33.

trained and prepared to function in our Spirit-assigned ministry. In order for believers to assume an effective place in every-member ministry, they must respond proactively to the Spirit's initiation. I have known church members who envisioned ways they could contribute to the work of their congregation but failed to do so because their pastor did not give them a specific invitation to serve. For instance, a person who has been graced with the gift of hospitality should not wait until they get a phone call, letter, or personal invitation from the pastor. They should involve themselves in a hospitality ministry of the local church, such as spending time with foster children who have aged out of the foster-care system.[2]

As one reflects on the apostle Paul's phrase "the body of Christ," this truth becomes clearer. A person's head does not need to communicate with the elbow in order to tell the foot to move. Likewise, since the Lord is the head of the church, he is able to assign ministries to individual members himself without consulting the local clergy or committee persons.

First Corinthians 12:1–11 reveals Paul's overall theology influencing his view of spiritual gifts. He affirms his belief that "life in the present is conditioned by the life of the future that has already begun with Christ's death and resurrection (cf. 4:1–5; 7:29–31); but that life has only begun, it is not yet consummated."[3] Therefore, a second nugget that we learn from 1 Corinthians 12 is that believers today, like the Corinthians, must nurture loving and responsible relationships with other believers. Their relationships will be properly nurtured as they

- participate in the mutual edification of one another through the use of spiritual gifting, which is utterly unlike the goals of individualistic spirituality;

- reject the notion that the benchmark of faithful membership is attendance at religious gatherings as spectators; and

---

2. This instruction is not intended to subvert the authority or guidance of the senior pastor. It does suggest, however, that a parishioner who requires a personal invitation by the pastor before they will serve, fails to heed the call of the Holy Spirit to minister by using their spiritual gift(s).

3. Fee, *First Epistle to the Corinthians*, 573.

- grasp the fact that the Christian life goes beyond having one's own spiritual and physical needs met by the Lord.

As we have seen, the Holy Spirit graces believers with spiritual gifts for the sole purpose of their serving one another in the Christian community. A believer who uses his or her spiritual gift(s) for self-aggrandizement, or who refuses to offer their gift(s) to other believers, fails to function as the Spirit intended within the community of faith.

A third nugget that we learn from 1 Corinthians 12:1–11 is that the Spirit distributes gifts as he pleases, not as we deserve. Thus, presence of a spiritual gift in a believer reveals nothing about the believer's longevity in the faith, faithfulness, or spirituality. Spiritual gifts are not merit badges; they are not given as evidence of one's spiritual status in the church. Neophyte Christians may possess just as many (or even more) spiritual gifts than Christians who have been a part of the Way for a long time; however, this does not mean that the new Christian is more highly favored or the older Christian less favored by the Lord. In view of the fact that the Spirit sovereignly determines who is entrusted with a particular gift, we should resist the temptation to hunger for the status that some people associate with certain gifts. We should instead nurse an insatiable hunger to benefit the Body with the gifts God has graciously provided to us.

A fourth nugget that we learn from 1 Corinthians 12:1–11 is that the Spirit graces the community with spiritual gifts by distributing them to a variety of persons. No one believer is graced with every gift necessary for a congregation to function as the Spirit desires. The Spirit who manifests himself in a variety of ways distributes his gifts to various individuals across the church. By the Spirit's design, no one person can fulfill all the tasks, duties, and responsibilities of the church. The church hinges upon the trusting and loving interdependence of its members. This is how Christ intended it to function.

Accordingly, when a believer refuses to fellowship and worship with other believers, that believer fails to achieve the purpose that the Spirit intended for them. Every-member ministry requires the rejection of a holy hermit lifestyle. Blomberg emphasizes this point as he writes,

"All of Paul's emphasis on unity within diversity calls into question the behavior of growing numbers of Americans who claim to be religious, believe in God and even Christ, and yet drop out of organized church life or at least fade to its periphery."[4] Christians around the world must demonstrate that Christianity is "not merely a personal religion but fundamentally corporate."[5]

A fifth nugget that we learn from 1 Corinthians 12:1–11 is that Christians should properly value all spiritual gifts the Holy Spirit provides. Witherington suggests, "Paul would tell us that just as 'charismania,' an overemphasis on prophecy or tongues, is not healthy, neither is 'charisphobia,' the anathematizing of all such gifts."[6] While a congregation may grow accustomed to a certain group of manifestations, it should not exalt the regularly occurring gifts over those that occur less frequently and vice versa. The entire church should rejoice over the beneficial use of all spiritual gifts within its assembly. Furthermore, one cannot conclude with certainty that God desires each congregation to have every spiritual gift. While every church should welcome every gift the Spirit provides, "the slogan 'seek *all* the gifts,' is precisely what Paul never articulates!"[7]

---

4. Blomberg, *1 Corinthians*, 254.

5. Ibid.

6. Witherington, *Conflict and Community in Corinth*, 263.

7. Blomberg, *1 Corinthians*, 256.

QUIZ 2
Gifts of the Spirit

Next to each statement write *T* for true or *F* for false.

_____ 1. Most Christian believers have at least one spiritual gift.

_____ 2. The possession of spiritual gifts means all believers have the potential to be exemplary disciples.

_____ 3. The presence of a believer's spiritual gift reminds us of the Spirit's care and concern for the entire church.

_____ 4. Regardless of their gifts, women do not belong in ministry.

_____ 5. Typically, Christians should wait until they are asked or assigned to a task by a clergy person before exercising their spiritual gift.

_____ 6. The main objective for a Christian is to have their spiritual and physical needs met by the Lord.

_____ 7. A believer who refuses to offer their spiritual gifts to other believers falls short of the function the Spirit intended for them to have within the community of faith.

_____ 8. The presence of a spiritual gift in a believer is not linked with the believer's longevity in the faith, faithfulness, or spirituality.

_____ 9. Mature Christians should be embarrassed when they see that a new Christian possess more gifts than they do.

_____ 10. No single believer is graced with every gift necessary for a congregation to function as the Spirit desires.

Further Reflection:

If the people of your church were to evaluate your spiritual effectiveness, according to Jesus' standards, how effective would they say you are?

CHAPTER 3

Spiritual Gifts Defined and Distinguished

Objectives
1. Examine in more depth what a spiritual gift is.
2. Contrast what a spiritual gift is with what it is not.
3. Be able to articulate specific characteristics of a spiritual gift.

In his book *Dynamics of Spiritual Gifts*, William McRae defines a spiritual gift as a "divine endowment of a special ability for service upon a member of the body of Christ."[1] Christian Schwarz defines a spiritual gift as "a special ability that God gives, according to his grace, to each member of the body of Christ to be used for the development of the kingdom."[2]

Although both definitions are true, I prefer Schwarz's because it contains five elements that truly capture the essence of a spiritual gift. First, a spiritual gift is a *special ability*. Every Christian should not be expected to possess every spiritual gift because each Christian, along with their spiritual gifting, provides a unique contribution to the Body. Schwarz comments, "Just as the human body has a variety of members

1. McRae, *Dynamics of Spiritual Gifts*, 18.
2. Schwarz, *3 Colors of Ministry*, 42.

and organs, so the body of Christ—the church—is comprised of a great variety of Christians, each of whom has his or her own special function (cf. Rom. 12:4–8, 1 Cor. 12:17–20)."[3]

Second, a spiritual gift is something that *God gives*. Although a Christian may desire a particular gift, one will only possess it if the Spirit decides to grace them with it. The Holy Spirit cannot be manipulated into giving a person a spiritual gift because they desire it, have studied its use, or have been trained in the use of that specific gift. In addition, no one has the right to boast about their possession of a particular spiritual gift, because the Spirit provided the gift. Paul addressed this issue in 1 Corinthians 12–14. One can safely conclude that some of the members in the Corinthian church bragged about their gift of tongues, apparently believing they were more spiritual than those who had not been graced with the gift of tongues. Paul, however, corrected this false notion.

Third, Schwarz's definition points toward the fact that a spiritual gift demonstrates God's *grace*. As we noted earlier, God does not provide a gift as a sign of the believer's merit, favor, or spiritual maturity. While neophyte Christians may be more gifted than those who have been disciples for twenty-five years, the effectiveness of their spiritual gifts will still depend on their spiritual maturity and the training they have received in using them. Schwarz writes, "I have met many individuals whom God abundantly blessed with spiritual gifts immediately after their conversion, and because they were so young in their faith, they used them quite immaturely."[4]

Fourth, Schwarz's definition makes clear that *every believer* is graced by the Holy Spirit with a spiritual gift. A Christian may not realize what their particular gift is or how to use that gift; however, this does not negate the fact that they possess a gift. Furthermore, everyone who has a spiritual gift has been designated by God to serve in ministries related to that gift. For example, if you have been graced with the spiritual gift of teaching, it means God intends for you to function in ministries in which one teaches. You will find a variety of ministries

---

3. Ibid.
4. Schwarz, *3 Colors of Ministry*, 42.

in the church that depend on this gift, such as Sunday school classes, small groups, youth tutoring sessions, addiction prevention and relief programs, and a host of others.

Fifth, God supplies spiritual gifts *for the benefit of the whole church*. While the individual Christian possesses a particular gift, it is intended for the church and must be used for the good of all. Schwarz's definition captures the heart of 1 Corinthians 12:4–7, "There are different kinds of gifts, but the same Spirit. There are different kinds of service, but the same Lord. There are different kinds of working, but the same God works all of them in all men. Now to each one the manifestation of the Spirit is given for the common good."

Believers also need to understand what spiritual gifts are not. First, spiritual gifts must be distinguished from natural talents. Talents are abilities given by the Lord to believers and unbelievers alike "to benefit mankind on a natural level."[5] As a result, talents can be found throughout humanity, whereas spiritual gifts are exclusive to the body of Christ. For instance, a person with the talent to draw great pictures might be a disciple of Christ, an atheist, or an agnostic. The spiritual gift of craftsmanship, however, can only be found in Christian circles. While talents tend to benefit the world and mankind in general, spiritual gifts primarily benefit the body of Christ and contribute toward its health. Reiterated, talents are given by God and purposed to benefit the world, while spiritual gifts are given by God and purposed to benefit his kingdom.

McRae writes, "Power and blessing are missing where there is natural talent only. Even a believer may have a talent without a gift."[6] Charles Bryant further develops this thought in his book *Rediscovering Our Spiritual Gifts*: "The biblical idea of charismatism has a spiritual-nonphysical attribute that other physical and mental traits do not have. Simply because a person appears to have, or actually displays, an unusual physical or mental adroitness does not mean that he or she has the Spirit power necessary for building up the body of Christ."[7]

---

5. McRae, *Dynamics of Spiritual Gifts*, 20.

6. Ibid., 21.

7. Bryant, *Rediscovering Our Spiritual Gifts*, 34.

For example, a church member may be able to give excellent speeches, but if that person is not gifted by the Holy Spirit to prophesy, she/he will not be as effective in proclaiming the gospel as a person who is so endowed. For example, the talented speaker may persuade many young people in church or community gatherings to keep away from drugs. Such a person may also promote righteous action by speaking on public policy issues within their community. Indeed, such a person who does not possess the spiritual gift of prophecy may even preach the gospel effectively on a particular occasion; however, over the long run a member of the Body gifted to prophesy will be more successful in spurring spiritual growth. While natural talent is sufficient in many situations, we should make every effort to offer both our spiritual gifts and natural talents to the Lord.

Second, we must be careful not to mistake the fruit of the Spirit for spiritual gifts. As Paul writes in Galatians 5:22–23, "The fruit of the Spirit is love, joy, peace, patience, kindness, goodness, faithfulness, gentleness, and self-control." Even a new creation in Christ can bear the fruit of the Spirit. All Christians, regardless of their God-assigned gifts and ministries, should evidence the fruit of the Spirit in their lives. However, the gifts of the Spirit will determine how effectively we accomplish what we attempt to do for, with, and through Christ. Any maturing Christian will display the fruit of the Spirit, but that is not true of spiritual gifts, because a Christian may refuse, misuse, or stifle his or her gifts. As Bryant states, "The fruit of the Spirit is what *we are*...The gifts of the Spirit are what *we do*."[8]

Third, we must understand how spiritual gifts are different from our Christian duties. Christian Schwarz articulates it this way, "Universal Christian responsibilities apply to all Christians, regardless of whether or not they might be gifted in those areas. Every spiritual gift corresponds to a universal responsibility."[9] Not all of us have spiritual gifts related to Christian duties, but that does not excuse us from our responsibility.

---

8. Ibid., 40.

9. Schwarz, *3 Colors of Ministry*, 48.

For example, every Christian is required to have faith, but those with the spiritual gift of faith will exhibit extraordinary faith and thus tend to have their prayers answered in extraordinary ways and frequency. Likewise, all Christians are called to tell others about their experience with Christ. Members of the Body with the spiritual gift of evangelism, however, are more likely to lead someone to Christ as they tell others about him. Spiritual gifts help some of us to carry out the Great Commission and Great Commandments more effectively than others. However, we should not allow the absence of a particular spiritual gift to discourage us from carrying out these duties.

Fourth, a spiritual gift is not something to seek for the purpose of self-fulfillment. Personal fulfillment will occur as a result of using one's gift; however, fulfillment must not be the goal of using one's gift. Since the Holy Spirit graces a person with a gift to edify the church, our primary concern with respect to any spiritual gift must be to lovingly enrich other believers. Paul alludes to this when he writes, "If I speak in the tongues of men or of angels, but do not have love, I am only a resounding gong or a clanging cymbal. If I have the gift of prophecy and can fathom all mysteries and all knowledge, and if I have a faith that can move mountains, but do not have love, I am nothing. If I give all I possess to the poor and give over my body to hardship that I may boast, but do not have love, I gain nothing" (1 Cor 13:1–3 NIV).

On the other hand, a member of the Body who feels miserable while serving in a particular ministry must not be involved in the ministry indicated by their spiritual gift(s). While it is true that any spiritual gift may entail a degree of burdensome work, exercising one's gift should ultimately bring a measure of joy and fulfillment. For example, a gifted teacher may endure a rigorous time of class preparation but will feel a sense of contentment while sharing the information with their students.

I have heard some people complain about serving in a particular ministry, although they spiritualized their discontentment as "bearing their cross." (Note that Jesus was not referring to misery in ministry when he declared, "Whoever wants to be my disciple must deny themselves and take up their cross and follow me" (Matt 16:24 NIV). He was referring to the fact that all of his disciples make a permanent decision to commit their lives to him.) Christians who feel no sense of satisfaction in their current ministry would enhance their lives, and the lives of others, by identifying their true spiritual gift(s) and relocating to their God-assigned ministry in the church.

Furthermore, when believers are intent upon edifying the church, they are less likely to be concerned with whether their gift is spotlighted. This should stifle the complaint: "No one will allow me to use my gift!" Believers who seek to edify the church will find ways to use their spiritual gifts in creative ways. For example, a Christian spiritually gifted to preach may not be invited to preach during Sunday morning worship services. This gifted person can, however, create a new ministry that addresses needs that their congregation does not currently meet —perhaps preaching in different setting, such as a nursing home or prison. Likewise, persons graced with the gift of healing need not wait for a public healing service to use this gift; they can visit members of the congregation at hospitals and nursing homes, and exercise their gift of healing there.

Finally, we should note that a spiritual gift is not a temporary empowerment. When the Holy Spirit distributes a spiritual gift to a believer, that person possesses the gift permanently. There may be times when a believer's spiritual gift becomes dormant. In other words, you may continue to possess a gift, although it is not the season to exercise your gift in the church. For example, a senior pastor may retire and join a different congregation. Although the occasion of using the gift of prophecy every Sunday has passed, this person still possesses the gift and can apply the gift if called upon to do so.

Significantly, this means that if a Christian exercises a spiritual gift in one congregation and relocates to a different church, they will not lose the spiritual gifts God conferred upon them. If the Holy Spirit desires for them to exercise their gift in the new setting, he will open doors of opportunity for them to do so. If a believer has a lapse in morality, this may also affect their ability to use their spiritual gift, causing the gift to be inactive. Even in this circumstance, when the person is restored, the Lord can make use of the gifting the Holy Spirit has already placed in them.

QUIZ 3
Gifts of the Spirit

Next to each answer write *T* for true or *F* for false.

_____ 1. A spiritual gift is any special or unique ability that a person uses for God's kingdom.

_____ 2. Every Christian is expected to make a standard contribution in order for the church to succeed.

_____ 3. No Christian has the right to boast about the possession of a particular spiritual gift.

_____ 4. A spiritual gift comes as a result of the time, education, and dedication a person invests in a certain area of the church.

_____ 5. A believer's spiritual gifts are evidence of that person's level of spiritual maturity.

_____ 6. The effectiveness of a spiritual gift may depend on a believer's spiritual maturity and whether or not they have been trained to use their gift.

_____ 7. A believer cannot possess a spiritual gift without knowing what the gift is or how to use it.

_____ 8. The Holy Spirit distributes spiritual gifts to benefit the church.

_____ 9. A spiritual gift is the same thing as a natural talent.

_____ 10. The exercise of a spiritual gift should be distinguished from demonstrating the fruit of the Spirit or fulfilling universal Christian duties.

Further Reflection:

Select another member of the church and share with them the characteristics of a spiritual gift in your own words.

CHAPTER 4
Spiritual Gift Discovery

Objectives
1. We will learn a seven-step spiritual gift discovery process.
2. We will consider the role of spiritual gifts in the life of a healthy congregation.

In his book *Your Spiritual Gifts Can Help Your Church Grow*, C. Peter Wagner observes, "One of the primary spiritual exercises for any Christian person is to discover, develop, and use his or her spiritual gift."[1] A question frequently asked by believers is, "How do I discover or identify my spiritual gifts?" In fact, one study revealed that 80 percent of all Christians could not name their spiritual gifts.[2] If you want to discover your spiritual gifts, you may benefit from the seven-step process of gift discovery described in this chapter.

The first step toward discovering your spiritual gift is to open your heart to the Lord in prayer.[3] Saturate the entire gift discovery process in prayer. Ask the Lord for wisdom with the confidence that he "gives [wisdom] generously to all without finding fault" (James 1:5). At the same

---

1. Wagner, *Your Spiritual Gifts*, 36.
2. Schwarz, *3 Colors of Ministry*, 55.
3. Ibid., 56.

time, pledge to offer your gift(s) to the Body as the Lord intends, and prepare yourself to accept what the Lord reveals. I recall a conversation with a Christian who took pride in the fact that he did not possess the gift of tongues. A more commendable approach is to be open to all gifts the Holy Spirit distributes and not to place a premium on the gifts one has received or not received. You may discover that you are not spiritually gifted in the areas you initially believed you were; conversely, the Lord may reveal that you have spiritual gifts that you never imagined. Therefore, as you begin to pray about this process, ask yourself two questions:

- Am I open to receiving any spiritual gifts that God may choose to give me, whether or not they are listed in the Bible?

- Are there any spiritual gifts that I would prefer not to have?

The second step in the gift discovery process is to commit yourself to using the gifts that God identifies in your life.[4] When you identify the spiritual gifts with which the Holy Spirit has graced you, you simultaneously identify the kind of ministries in which the Lord desires you to serve. A believer who identifies their spiritual gift(s) and fails to edify the church with their gift(s), or refuses to do so, falls short of their God-assigned purpose. What the apostle Peter wrote to the Christians of his day applies to every Christian today: "Each one should use whatever gift he has received to serve others, faithfully administering God's grace in its various forms" (1 Peter 4:10). Congregations in which a majority of the people are appropriately functioning as ministers by exercising their spiritual gifts are bound for kingdom success.

The third step toward gift identification is to educate yourself on the various ways in which the Holy Spirit graces individuals with gifts.[5] If you have little understanding about the various ways the Holy Spirit empowers Christians to minister, you will have a hard time identifying your own spiritual gift(s). Continue to learn as much as you can about spiritual gifts. This can be accomplished in a variety of ways, such as

---

4. Ibid., 57.
5. Ibid., 58.

- studying the spiritual gifts specifically listed in the Bible,

- observing spiritual gifts that God gives to the body of Christ that are not specifically listed in the Bible,

- speaking with a wide range of individuals who have identified their spiritual gifts and asking them about their gift discovery process,

- reading popular and scholarly literature on spiritual gifts, and

- making an appointment with a spiritual gifts coach. This is often a pastor or ministry leader in your local congregation who has a clear understanding of the gifts of the Spirit and is charged by God to help people find their place in ministry.

The fourth step is to take a spiritual gift identification test. These tests can be accessed through your pastoral staff or a spiritual gifts coach, if your congregation has one.[6] A wide range of spiritual gift discovery instruments are available at Christian bookstores or on the Internet. Examples can be found in Christian Schwarz's *The 3 Colors of Ministry*, published by ChurchSmart Resources (Saint Charles, IL); C. Peter Wagner's *Your Spiritual Gifts Can Help Your Church Grow*, published by Regal Books (Ventura, CA); and *Uniquely You*, by Mels Carbonell and Stanley Ponz, available from Warner Press (Anderson, IN). All of these include questions that pertain to the spiritual gifts listed in the Bible, and some consider other manifestations of the Spirit that Scripture does not specifically classify as spiritual gifts. Whichever instrument you use, be careful to scrutinize the results in light of the other six steps outlined in this chapter.[7]

---

6. Additional information about the ministry of spiritual gifts coaches is available in the Equipper's Guide, which is a component of the New Life Together package for group study.

7. For instance, a spiritual gift inventory may suggest that a person has the spiritual gift of teaching. If members of the church, however, are not able to learn when that person attempts to teach, it may invalidate the results of the spiritual gift inventory.

The fifth step is to try using an assortment of spiritual gifts.[8] It is difficult to know with certainty whether you have been graced with a specific gift until you put it into practice. For this reason, church leaders should create opportunities for local members to safely employ a wide range of spiritual gifts in the congregation's ministry. Use of some spiritual gifts entails greater risks; if possible, those gifts should be tried in smaller settings. For example, if a person believes he may have the spiritual gift of preaching, he should not experiment with this gift during a Sunday morning service. Experimentation can take place during a small Bible-study class, cell-group meeting, or a Sunday school setting. This method allows the believer to test the use of this spiritual gift while minimizing potential embarrassment.

Step six is to verify effectiveness of your gift(s).[9] Since the Holy Spirit empowers believers to do kingdom work by gracing them with spiritual gifts, one indication of the presence of a particular gift is whether its exercise produces the intended result. Schwarz comments, "If you have the gift of healing, you will see others restored to health. If you have the gift of teaching, others will learn from you. If you have the gift of leadership, others will follow you...Spirit gifts are given to produce results; thus, the evaluation of your effectiveness is a vital step in the gift discovery process."[10] If you discover that you are regularly ineffective in an area of ministry, this may indicate you should withdraw from that activity and move to a ministry for which you are better equipped. It is a greater disservice to the Lord, to yourself, and to your local congregation to persist in a ministry where you are not spiritually gifted to serve than to allow that particular ministry to remain inactive until the church identifies person(s) spiritually gifted to carry out the task.

However, be aware of at least two exceptions to the test of effectiveness. First, a Christian graced with a specific spiritual gift may be ineffective for lack of training. This is a primary reason to continually strive to learn more about the gifts you have received. The second exception

---

8. Schwarz, *3 Colors of Ministry*, 61.
9. Ibid., 62.
10. Ibid.

has to do with our humanity fallibility. Even when endowed with spiritual gifts, no Christian can expect to be utterly perfect in ministry at all times. On occasion, any member of the Body may fail in the use of a spiritual gift; this alone does not prove that they lack that particular gift. Only if they are customarily ineffective in the exercise of a certain gift do we see evidence that they have not been graced in that way.

The seventh step in the spiritual gifts discovery process is to seek the validation of other believers. Since the Holy Spirit distributes spiritual gifts for the edification of the body of Christ, the members of the Body are in the best position to confirm whether a certain spiritual gift is evident. If you are convinced that you have a particular spiritual gift but your congregation is unable to confirm and affirm that you do, the chances are great that you do not have that gift. Schwarz's comment on this subject proves helpful:

I know Christians who are 100 percent convinced that God has blessed them with a certain gifts. They have prayed intensely about it, in fact, this kind of prayer is one of their favorite activities; they are ready to apply the gift (whether it is appropriate or not); they know all about the hidden secrets behind the gift (usually far more than you can find in the Bible);…they have experimented a lot (being really risky and not caring whether or not some of their experiments have done harm); and they perceive their ministry as being extremely effective. The problem is that they are the only ones that see it that way.[11]

I was pastor of a person who was absolutely convinced they had a particular gift and continually asked permission to demonstrate the gift publically. My knowledge of the individual (and, more importantly, the collective unwillingness of the congregation to allow this individual to demonstrate that particular gift) suggested to me that the gift wasn't there. When a person uses spiritual gifts allotted to them by the Spirit and functions effectively in a ministry where those gifts must be used,

---

11. Ibid.

the congregation will gladly affirm the authenticity of those gifts and be abundantly blessed. Moreover, when the Holy Spirit graces an individual with a spiritual gift that must be publicly expressed—such as preaching, teaching, or artistic performance—that person can rest assured that God who gave them the gift will open doors of opportunity for the expression of that gift when the timing is appropriate. As a young minister, I was taught never to ask anyone for permission to preach because "my gift would make room for me." I have fully adhered to this principle, and over the past ten years I have preached in more than forty different congregations, chapels, and conventions— some multiple times—across the United States and in Africa. It is my experience that the Spirit will open the doors of opportunity according to the gifts he grants. We need only to focus on sharpening our gifts so we are prepared when those doors of opportunity fly open.

Do not feel discouraged or embarrassed if you discover that you are not gifted as you originally perceived. Instead be encouraged because you are one step closer to finding the spiritual gifts and ministries God intends for you. When you resign from a position where you are not equipped to serve, you can know the hope, anticipation, and excitement associated with finding the place of service that God has designated for you in the body of Christ.

As members of your church identify spiritual gifts with which the Spirit has graced them, you can expect four aspects of your congregation's ministry to grow in importance: (1) worship, (2) Bible study, (3) prayer, and (4) evidence of God's power.[12]

Worship will grow in importance because it will become more than a private experience. Christ's followers will connect with other members of the body of Christ during worship. Charles V. Bryant writes:

> The human body is healthy only when all parts and systems work in harmony for mutual benefits. Similarly, the Body of Christ in worship is healthy only when all parts (members) as gifts share their energy with and for the benefit of the others.

---

12. Bryant, *Rediscovering Our Spiritual Gifts*, 27.

The church at authentic worship requires the presence and operation of all the gifts, not just those operated by the minister and the musicians. When the church is so assembled, no force in the world can withstand its power for good (see Matthew 16:18).

Worship becomes more exciting when parishioners come together and use their spiritual gifts during worship. If one leaves such a service without a renewed or recharged sense of continuing fellowship in ministry under Christ, it is to fall short of what true worship offers. The wise leader will want to engage as many gifts as possible.[13]

Bible study will grow in importance as believers identify their spiritual gifts because Scripture will take on new meaning. Bryant writes, "The Bible will take on a new authority, not as a reservoir of unquestioned doctrines, but as a divinely inspired corrective for human error and a cure for apathy and false enthusiasm."[14] For Christians dedicated to using their spiritual gifts to edify the church, Scripture will stand as the definitive guide for avoiding abuse and ineffectiveness.

The significance of prayer increases, because believers will need to solicit God's will and direction. Prayer will prepare them emotionally and spiritually for the work they aspire to do in the kingdom. Consequently, "gift consciousness often delivers many persons from predominantly asking God for things to giving praise and thanksgiving. Much of their praying is for guidance to use the gifts in humility and gratitude."[15]

While believers need training in the use of their gifts, the power that enables them to use their gifts effectively comes from God alone. In a real sense, "knowing and doing God's will is impossible without God's power that accompanies the faithful use of gifts. It is possible for us to be all that we can be without any direct or conscious reliance on God. It is impossible for us to be *more* than we are without God's

---

13. Ibid., 27–28.

14. Ibid.

15. Ibid., 29.

presence and power."[16] As believers worship, read Scripture, and pray, they will come in contact with the power source they need to be effective in ministry.

---

16. Ibid., 30.

QUIZ 4
Gifts of the Spirit

Next to each statement, write *T* for true or *F* for false.

_____ 1. Discovering and using one's spiritual gifts is essential to the spiritual journey of a Christian.

_____ 2. Prayer is only essential after a person has discovered their spiritual gift(s).

_____ 3. Believers are not truly ready to discover their spiritual gifts unless they are receptive to God's will for their lives.

_____ 4. A believer who has discovered her or his spiritual gift(s) should withhold them from the church if other church members cannot be trusted.

_____ 5. Learning about the various spiritual gifts that the Spirit distributes will assist you in discovering your own spiritual gifts.

_____ 6. Conversations with other believers about spiritual gifting do not advance the process of gift discovery.

_____ 7. A spiritual gift assessment or test is all you need to identify your gift.

_____ 8. Experimenting with a possible spiritual gift will surely lead to embarrassment.

_____ 9. Effective use of a gift over time indicates the genuine presence of that gift.

_____ 10. Since spiritual gifts are given for the edification of the Body, the church's confirmation of that gift is very important.

Further Reflection:
As a result of hearing the gift discovery steps I will…

CHAPTER 5

Headship of Christ

Objectives

1. Recognize the implications of Christ's being the Head of the church.
2. Gain a renewed sense of urgency in serving the underprivileged.
3. Identify community problems that we will seek to address with other members of our congregation.

In his letter to the Ephesians, the apostle Paul addressed a group of Gentile Christians in order to instruct them on "how to live out their distinctively Christian identity."[1] He emphasizes the consequences of Christian identity and the fact that Christ is the Head of the church. For example, he writes, "Wives, submit to your husbands as to the Lord. For the husband is the head of the wife as Christ is the head of the church, his body, of which he is the Savior. Now as the church submits to Christ, so also wives should submit to their husbands in everything" (Eph 5:22–24).[2]

---

1. Wimmer, "Equipping the Saints for Service," 81.
2. See also Ephesians 1:22; 4:15; 5:23; and Colossians 2:18–19.

In order to fully understand the biblical concept of the priesthood of believers and every-member ministry, we must recognize that Jesus Christ is the Head, not only of the universal church, but also of all local congregations. Christ himself rules your congregation. Christ is the chief executive officer, commander-in-chief, and chief operations officer of your local church. The immediate implications of this are threefold.

First, no individual within your congregation has a legitimate claim to be the church's head. The public often incorrectly attributes human ownership to local congregations. For example, people casually refer to Metropolitan Church of God in Detroit, Michigan, as "Pastor Earley's church" or Covenant Faith Church of God in Chicago, Illinois, as "Pastor Chin's church." However, "no church leader in the New Testament is ever called the head of a local body. That title is reserved for Christ."[3] As a result, every church leader—including bishops, pastors, and trustee chairpersons—must carry out the will of Christ. No human leader is to ever guide a local congregation according to his or her own plans. In fact, "When the Body acts apart from the head, it is because of disease, handicap, injury, or some malfunction. When the church's actions contradict the ways and will of Christ, it is because of some disorder or malfunction within the body politic."[4]

Second, the members of any local congregation are to receive their marching orders from the Head of the church, Jesus Christ. He has not delegated to leaders of local congregations the responsibility to appoint or recruit parishioners to serve in specific ministries. Moreover, "the head does not tell the hand to tell the foot what to do. The head is directly connected to the foot. Therefore, people find their ministries not by being directed by the leaders but by being motivated and equipped by the Head."[5] Every believer must proactively seek to discern what Christ, the Head, has for them to accomplish. Disciples of Christ need not wait until some member of the pastoral staff calls them to a certain place of ministry. Ideally, when a church member believes they have

---

3. Ogden, *Unfinished Business*, 49.

4. Robert O. Dulin Jr., "Walking Through the Book of Colossians: The Preeminent Christ," midweek Bible study handout for the Metropolitan Church of God, September 25, 2007.

5. Ogden, *Unfinished Business*, 49.

discerned their spiritual gifting, that person will approach the pastoral staff to confirm the existence of that spiritual gift and obtain guidance in the proper use of it.

Third, as we identify the spiritual gifts we have received and the ministries to which we have been assigned, we must understand that Christ expects us to imitate him by "living according to the norms of the dawning kingdom—a kingdom where the poor would receive justice, and peace would prevail."[6] The church continues the earthly ministry of Christ through its involvement in evangelism and social action. In other words, the church extends Christ's ministry to people's spiritual and physical dimensions.

This responsibility grows out of the biblical teaching about sin. Many congregations across the United States preach that our holy God hates sin. Not all churches, however, readily articulate that sin is both personal and social. Ron Sider writes, "Again and again, the prophets make it clear that we sin both by lying, stealing, and committing adultery, and also by participating in unjust legal and economic systems without doing what God wants to change them."[7] Therefore, in order for the good news of the kingdom to be realized, the church must deal with both personal sin and structural sin through evangelism and social action.

Evangelism alone does not address the ills of society. Throughout the course of church history, many sincere believers have participated in society's sinful structures. In fact, those sinful structures can enable Christians to engage in dishonorable behavior. For example, authentic Christians lived in the segregated South and participated in its practices. Their being "born again," in and of itself, did not move them to stop participating in the sinful practice of segregation. However, the Holy Spirit enabled certain Christian men and women to recognize the sinfulness of segregation and motivated them to work toward eliminating the injustice it caused in society. They worked outside of the walls of the church to make a difference. Their work would not

---

6. Sider, *Scandal of the Evangelical Conscience*, 62.
7. Sider, *Good News and Good Works*, 74.

have gone far enough had they only succeeded in stopping Christians from participating in segregation; society itself needed to be changed.

Social action addresses the structural sins of society as evangelism addresses personal sin. Persons must submit their lives to Christ and experience the transformation that he brings in order to fully participate in his kingdom. Moreover, anyone who seeks eternal life must not only receive Christ as their forgiving Priest but also as Prophet to instruct them and King to rule their lives. As Jesus states in Matthew 16:24, "Whoever wants to be my disciple must deny themselves and take up their cross and follow me" (NIV).

Christians must take evangelism seriously. Darryl B. Starnes Sr., writes, "There is no doubt that the Apostle Paul saw evangelism as a way of life. For him new life in Christ meant more than simply enjoying the benefits of reconciliation with God. It meant becoming an ambassador for Christ, entrusted with the ministry and the message of reconciliation. It meant a lifelong ministry of compelling people to be reconciled to God through Jesus Christ."[8]

Douglas M. Cecil of Dallas Theological Seminary aptly describes evangelism as "the communication of the good news of Jesus Christ—that He died for our sins and rose again—with the intent of inviting the listener to trust Christ. Evangelism is telling the Good News for the purpose of inviting the sinner to salvation."[9] Consequently, evangelism has two components: (1) sharing information about Jesus Christ, and (2) inviting the hearer to become a disciple of Jesus Christ. We must resist the notion that we can do evangelism by simply living a godly life in front of our neighbors. When we have entered the kingdom of God, we must begin to articulate our faith in Christ and our beliefs about Christ to nonbelievers, especially in light of the fact that "faith comes from hearing the message, and the message is heard through the word about Christ" (Rom 10:17 NIV).

Evangelism is accomplished as we obey the Great Commission and plant seeds of gospel truth, water those seeds, or reap a spiritual harvest. We plant seeds when we articulate gospel truths to nonbelievers,

---

8. Starnes, "Equipping the Saints," 98.
9. Cecil, *7 Principles of an Evangelistic Life*, 36.

introducing it into their hearts. If we invite our listeners to become disciples of Jesus at this point, we are likely to be rejected. We water seeds when we reaffirm the truth that has already been planted in their hearts. Once again, our nonbelieving friends may not choose to follow Jesus. When a Christian reaps a spiritual harvest, the nonbeliever accepts the invitation to discipleship, experiences rebirth, and begins a lifelong journey with Jesus as his or her Lord.[10] It should be noted that when a Christian starts an evangelistic conversation with a nonbeliever, they may not know whether they will plant, water, or reap a spiritual harvest, although the gospel truth they share is exactly the same.

The church's responsibility to address personal sin and structural sin becomes clear as we examine how Christ defines the gospel. Whereas some may understand the gospel primarily as the forgiveness of sins, the gospel Jesus preached "includes the fact that the messianic reign has in fact begun and there is now a reconciling community whose visible life is a powerful sign of the kingdom that has already begun and will some day arrive in its fullness."[11]

Ron Sider has articulated seven differences between the popular reductionist version of the gospel and Jesus' version. If the gospel is not just the forgiveness of sins but the good news of the kingdom: (1) We cannot separate a reconciled relationship with God and reconciled relationships with our brothers and sisters in Christ; whole relationships with other children of God are not optional. (2) We must understand that reconciled social and economic relationships in the body of Christ are a part of salvation; the removal of social barriers and sharing economically are essential in the life of a disciple. (3) We must understand more clearly that ministering to both physical and spiritual needs of people is not optional but essential to the gospel—for instance, people need both Jesus and a job. (4) We must see more vividly that the Christian community will always challenge the wrong of the status quo; the community of God will always be a countercultural, a loving critic of society. (5) Any sharing of the gospel that does not include a significant concern for human dignity, social empowerment, and economic justice for the

---

10. See 1 Corinthians 3:5–9.
11. Starnes, "Equipping the Saints," 76.

disenfranchised falls short of the true gospel. (6) We perceive more clearly that there must always be a sharp distinction between the church and the world; the body of Christ must resist the temptation to reflect the values of the world surrounding it. And (7) we cannot share the gospel through preaching alone; we must also live the gospel—in both word and deed.[12]

Ron Sider, Philip Olson, and Heidi Unruth outline the importance of addressing both personal sin and structural sin in their book *Churches That Make a Difference*. First, "social ministry provides a vehicle or foundation for spiritual nurture."[13] The social ministry of a congregation should draw people toward ministries that they would otherwise have never come in contact with. Consequently, social action provides opportunities for relationships to be established and for the gospel to be shared. When one's physical needs are met, that person is better positioned to have spiritual needs met as well. Social ministry also helps people experience the hand and the face of Christ through those who minister in his name. Additionally, social action helps the community understand that the church does indeed address relevant issues.

Second, "evangelism enhances the outcomes of social ministry."[14] A congregation's evangelistic ministry provides new hope, motivation, and self-esteem. It frees people from their spiritual bondage. Genuine Christian evangelism transforms people from victims to overcomers.

Thirdly, evangelism builds the church's capacity for social ministry. Evangelism that successfully adds people to the body of Christ increases the community of dedicated servants of Christ. Those who have experienced God's deliverance are often the most enthusiastic about offering hope to others. The testimony of new people joining the community of faith can motivate the congregation to stay on the path of social action. Furthermore, evangelism leads the wealthy to dedicate their resources to helping the poor.

Overall, Sider, Olson, and Unruth contend that "spiritual and social ministry, when woven together, yield a stronger fabric than either strand alone."[15]

---

12. Sider, *Good News and Good Works*, 78.
13. Sider, Olson, and Unruh, *Churches That Make a Difference*, 57.
14. Ibid., 58.
15. Ibid., 57.

QUIZ 5
Gifts of the Spirit

Next, to each statement, write *T* for true or *F* for false.

_____ 1. Jesus Christ is the commander-in-chief of the church worldwide.

_____ 2. Your pastor's congregation has the ability to be the greatest change agent the world has ever seen.

_____ 3. A congregation without Christ is similar to a chicken with its head cut off. It may run for a while, but eventually it will fall.

_____ 4. It is a pastor's responsibility to recruit members of the church to serve in specific ministries.

_____ 5. Churches involved in social action are more likely to be successful in their evangelistic efforts.

_____ 6. Authentic Christian ministry involves both evangelism and social action.

_____ 7. A Christian should not mix their political decisions with their spiritual convictions.

_____ 8. Biblically, unjust social structures are just as bad as individual moral transgressions, such as stealing, idolatry, and murder.

_____ 9. If more people were born again, that would cure the sinful structures of society.

_____ 10. Christians should focus solely on sharing the gospel and let the government deal with problems of human dignity, social empowerment, and economic justice.

Further Reflection:

What social justice issues would you like to partner with other church members to address?

CHAPTER 6

Threats to Be Avoided

Objectives

1. We will identify several threats to effective ministry.

2. We will learn how our leaders can guard against these threats and effect change if they identify such problems.

3. We will learn to value the cohesiveness we have with other believers.

Throughout the Bible we find that the Lord expects us to love him with all our heart, soul, and strength (Deut 6:5). He also expects us to love one another (John 13:34). Within the church we must have right relationships with God and righteous dealings with each other in order to function as the Lord intends.

Disorder and disunity can thwart our efforts to accomplish our God-given assignments. In other words, when the relationship between us and other believers is dysfunctional, it stifles our ability to offer our spiritual gifts to one another effectively.

What kind of things should we guard against in order to function as the Lord intends? First Corinthians 12:7–26 answers this question.[1]

---

1. The full text of 1 Corinthians 12 is available in Appendix A.

This lesson will explore five things that threaten the potential of a local congregation.

The first threat is *inactivity*. First Corinthians 12:4–11 lists several manifestations of the Spirit that often are called spiritual gifts. When an individual receives Christ as Lord, that person becomes a member of the church. The Spirit of God then graces that person with at least one spiritual gift, a special ability they are to use to benefit the body of Christ.

Every believer—no matter who they are, how long they have been saved, or what they have been saved from—is graced with a spiritual gift. The Spirit of God distributes these gifts to individual Christians to edify the body of Christ. To assume our rightful place in every-member ministry, we should realize that no one is called to do nothing.

The threat of inactivity is not avoided by simply attending worship services and church events. Imagine a typical Bible study in which believers show up, learn, and leave. This ministry consists of one teacher and thirty-five students. In this scenario, only the teacher is actively ministering to others. The other thirty-five Christians are positioned to receive the ministry of the teacher—both to learn the content of the lesson and then practice it. After receiving the ministry of the teacher, each student should render their spiritual gifts to others as well. In a real sense, every child of God is called and equipped to render *and* receive Spirit-empowered ministry.

When one member fails to render his or her gift appropriately, the other members of the church are robbed of an opportunity to be blessed. So let us encourage one another to use our spiritual gifts and hold one another accountable, lest any of us succumb to the temptation of inactivity. May God deliver every congregation from lethargic believers!

The second threat is the mindset of *inferiority*. First Corinthians 12:12–20 states that the foot does not cease to be a part of the body simply because it is not a hand, nor does the ear cease being a part of the body since it is not an eye. Individual Christians have different spiritual gifts, so believers must avoid discrediting themselves or the spiritual gifts with which they have been graced. No one should suppose that they are unimportant in the life of a local congregation because they do not possess a particular spiritual gift. The Holy Spirit does not grace believers with insignificant or optional spiritual gifts. To reiterate, no believer is called to do nothing, nor is any believer good for nothing.

The third threat is the mindset of *independence*.[2] Imagine the predicament of a person with perfectly good eyes but no hands. What would happen if the person slipped on ice? How would the eyes be protected against the fall? What if dirt got into the eye? Obviously, an eye can be greatly assisted and protected by hands. Likewise, each member of the body of Christ depends on other members for care and protection, and there is no way for the members of the church to be completely healthy unless they rely on each other.

This is a primary reason why Christians should be loving, caring, and supportive of each other. As we have seen, all believers need the edification of one another's spiritual gifts; but if our relationships are damaged, we are less likely to benefit from those gifts and thus miss out on a blessing of God. Moreover, everyone graced with a gift needs other church members to render their gift effectively. Regardless of how well one can preach, if his or her relationships are damaged to the point that the congregation refuses to listen, then that gift becomes ineffective.

The fourth threat is the mindset of *envy*. First Corinthians 12:22–25 makes it clear God has given us these gifts according to his will, so there is no reason for me to envy your spiritual gift. Both of us must fight the temptation of wishing we possessed each other's gift. This temptation is particularly felt with regard to publicly exercised gifts, such as preaching or prophecy. Some people tend to glorify these spiritual gifts rendered in public over the gifts that are not, but this Corinthian text articulates the truth that Christians who might seem to have less important functions in the body of Christ are actually indispensable. For example, some physical body parts would not normally be seen outside of a surgery room—organs such as hearts, lungs, or livers. Without these organs, however, no human being can live.

---

2. See 1 Corinthians 12:21.

Likewise, when it comes to the body of Christ, some saints exercise their spiritual gifts in secret, but they are indispensable!

The fifth threat is the mindset of *indifference* (see 1 Cor 12:26). Members of the body of Christ must be mindful of other members in the church. When one part of your body is injured, other parts feel the pain; in fact, that injury can make the rest of your body dysfunctional. If someone drops a heavy object on their foot, they probably would be in no mood to reconcile their checking account. Similarly, when someone in the church is hurting, other members of the body of Christ must take notice and tend to their needs. Charles Bryant comments, "Medical science defines sickness as a breakdown of communication and transmission of energy between the parts of the human body. It teaches further that nature designs and locates each part to serve the other parts. When any part is dysfunctional, the whole body suffers. The same is true about the church and its various functions."[3] Additionally, parishioners should celebrate with other church members when they celebrate. This proves that the community of faith knows how to appreciate its various spiritual gifts.

---

3. Bryant, *Rediscovering Our Spiritual Gifts*, 28.

QUIZ 6
Gifts of the Spirit

Next to each statement, write *T* for true or *F* for false.

_____ 1. The Lord requires his children to have a right relationship with him and with each other.

_____ 2. Disunity can distract believers from effectively rendering their gifts.

_____ 3. Spiritual gifts rendered in public are more important than spiritual gifts rendered privately.

_____ 4. Lethargic church members cause local congregations to achieve less than their potential.

_____ 5. The Lord has structured the church in such a way that individual members are able to function completely independent of each other while they do their ministry.

_____ 6. Since spiritual gifts are given by the Spirit, Christians' unhealthy personal relationships cannot hinder their use.

_____ 7. Members of the church should isolate themselves from one another when they experience tough times.

_____ 8. Christians must earn spiritual gifts that are publicly exercised.

_____ 9. Christians need each other in order to render their spiritual gifts.

_____ 10. When a member fails to render a gift, the whole church suffers.

Further Reflection:

Of the threats mentioned, which ones have you struggled with?

What will you do about it?

CHAPTER 7

Ministry According to Exodus 18:13–27

Objectives

1. We will explore the implications of Exodus 18:13–27 for a congregation.

2. We will celebrate the source of our spiritual power and ministerial authority.

3. We will refuse to place the full burden of ministry upon the pastoral staff.

There is more to this story—any biblical story—than meets the eye. Exodus 18 is as much a theological statement as anything else in the book. It is not simply reporting events, but reporting with a purpose."[1] Exodus 18:13–27 illustrates Israel's concern for "the establishment of stable procedures and due process, which will make justice everywhere available and reliable."[2] Additionally, it provides useful information for today's church leaders as they strive to encourage the ministry involvement of all members of the community of faith. Here is that text in full:

---

1. Enns, *Exodus*, 377.
2. Brueggemann, "Exodus," 827.

The next day Moses took his seat to serve as judge for the people, and they stood around him from morning till evening. When his father-in-law saw all that Moses was doing for the people, he said, "What is this you are doing for the people? Why do you alone sit as judge, while all these people stand around you from morning till evening?"

Moses answered him, "Because the people come to me to seek God's will. Whenever they have a dispute, it is brought to me, and I decide between the parties and inform them of God's decrees and laws."

Moses' father-in-law replied, "What you are doing is not good. You and these people who come to you will only wear yourselves out. The work is too heavy for you; you cannot handle it alone. Listen now to me and I will give you some advice, and may God be with you. You must be the people's representative before God and bring their disputes to him. Teach them the decrees and laws, and show them the way to live and the duties they are to perform. But select capable men from all the people—men who fear God, trustworthy men who hate dishonest gain—and appoint them as officials over thousands, hundreds, fifties and tens. Have them serve as judges for the people at all times, but have them bring every difficult case to you; the simple cases they can decide themselves. That will make your load lighter, because they will share it with you. If you do this and God so commands, you will be able to stand the strain, and all these people will go home satisfied."

Moses listened to his father-in-law and did everything he said. He chose capable men from all Israel and made them leaders of the people, officials over thousands, hundreds, fifties and tens. They served as judges for the people at all times. The difficult cases they brought to Moses, but the simple ones they decided themselves. Then Moses sent his father-in-law on his way, and Jethro returned to his own country.

The first lesson we learn from this text is that pastors cannot be solely responsible for the church's ministry. When they attempt to do so, the chances are great that they will burn out and the people will suffer. Exodus 18 and similar texts confirm that throughout the history of God's dealing with his people, he has never chosen to invest all of the spiritual resources that a community needs in one individual. Another Old Testament example is found at the end of Exodus as the tabernacle was being built. From the start, God let Moses know that a variety of individuals from the community would take part in the task of erecting the tabernacle (Ex 35–40).

Romans 12:6–8 stands as a clear New Testament statement of how God uses a variety of persons to accomplish his will:

> We have different gifts, according to the grace given us. If a man's gift is prophesying, let him use it in proportion to his faith. If it is serving, let him serve; if it is teaching, let him teach; if it is encouraging, let him encourage; if it is contributing to the needs of others, let him give generously; if it is leadership, let him govern diligently; if it is showing mercy, let him do it cheerfully.

An unhealthy church is one in which all roads lead to the pastor. Everything must come across his or her desk, and church members assume that the only person qualified to do the work of the Lord is the educated or ordained pastor. Unfortunately, a pastor who accepts this kind of role often will be applauded by the congregation.[3] Like Moses, any church leader who attempts to do work that should be spread throughout the community will become tired and ineffective.

This is why today's pastors must continually evaluate individuals for over- and under-functioning in order to identify and correct unwise actions and structures. Steven Wimmer wrote the following in his dissertation, *Equipping the Saints for Service*:

---

3. Ogden, *Unfinished Business*, 117.

The over and under functioning construct refers to the systemic balance that exists between the levels of functioning of a congregation's members. Some members (often leaders) *overfunction* by worrying, working, praying, giving and sacrificing much. While others *underfunction* by worrying, working, praying, giving and sacrificing little.[4]

In order for the church to avoid over- and under-functioning, pastors must behave in ways that evidence their awareness that they cannot do everything themselves and that the Holy Spirit is capable of gifting others to serve in ministry. Pastors must not cultivate the belief that they are indispensible.[5] As pastors refuse to carry the burden of ministry alone and train other leaders, they will enable others to render their God-given gifts as the Holy Spirit intended.

The second lesson we learn from this text is that today's pastor must accept God's call to equip other leaders for the work of ministry. Initially, Moses was the tool God used to carry out this enormous task; however, the task became too great for one man to do efficiently. God's command to Moses was to assume the role of an equipping leader. Moses was charged with equipping all of Israel with the knowledge of God's laws and equipping other leaders to join him in the essential ministry of judging. In other words, God commanded Moses to duplicate himself.

The practice of equipping and duplicating leaders is seen again in the book of Exodus as Israel built the tabernacle. The Lord choose Bezalel and Oholiah, two men he had gifted artistically, to design the sanctuary. Exodus 35:34 states that Bezalel and Oholiah had "the ability to teach others," so God chose leaders not only to lead but also to teach others, thus duplicating themselves.

Another illustration of equipping and duplication can be found in Ephesians 4:11–14 as it refers to the work of the Holy Spirit:

---

4. Wimmer, "Equipping the Saints for Service," 131.

5. Ogden, *Unfinished Business*, 117.

It was he who gave some to be apostles, some to be prophets, some to be evangelists, and some to be pastors and teachers, to prepare God's people for works of service, so that the body of Christ may be built up until we all reach unity in the faith and in the knowledge of the Son of God and become mature, attaining to the whole measure of the fullness of Christ. Then we will no longer be infants, tossed back and forth by the waves, and blown here and there by every wind of teaching and by the cunning and craftiness of men in their deceitful scheming.

In this text, the author of Ephesians encourages a specific group of church leaders to strive for specific results. Apostles, prophets, evangelists, pastors, and teachers will know that they have accomplished their job of equipping when "the saints are doing the work of ministry, the body of Christ is being built up, the whole body is attaining a unity in the faith, and the community together is expressing the full stature of Christ."[6]

Wimmer offers further insight on this principle that pastors must equip other members of the body of Christ to minister. He writes:

Christ has apportioned his gifts to each member of the body (Eph 4:7). The leaders [of the church] serve the church by equipping all the saints for ministry (Eph 4:11–12). These texts offer an alternative to the practices and structures of the church under the influence of Christendom, where the normative function of the laity is to be good citizens and follow the orders of the clergy. These texts also confront the assumptions beneath the principle of scarcity and abundance, where the few lay claim to the ministry that rightly belongs to the many. The vision that these texts inspire is one in which the calling and gifts of the laity are crucial.[7]

---

6. Ibid., 132.

7. Wimmer, "Equipping the Saints for Service," 171.

The third lesson we learn from Exodus 18:13–27 is tied to Israel's covenant law. God is the author of the law, provides its authority, and is ultimately the One who must interpret and apply it to Israel's daily life. Just as God was the source of Moses' knowledge and decisions, the newly duplicated leaders would provide decisions informed by God. Therefore, Israel could expect the same quality of decisions from the newly assigned judges as Moses made.

The same concept holds true for the Christian church today. Since pastors derive their wisdom and authority from God, the leaders they equip must do the same. Therefore, as pastors equip other leaders and so duplicate themselves, the community of faith can expect the quality of leadership that undeviating direction from God provides. In other words, "The starting point in equipping the church for mission is the liberating truth that God is the ultimate equipper: giving vision and gifts, empowering through the Spirit's presence, motivating and guiding."[8]

---

8. Stephens, *Other Six Days*, 209.

QUIZ 7
Gifts of the Spirit

Next to each statement, write *T* for true or *F* for false.

_____ 1. Pastors who endeavor to do the work of ministry by themselves should be appreciated and affirmed.

_____ 2. Only ordained clergy with a seminary education are qualified to render effective ministry.

_____ 3. A pastor can demonstrate his or her value by allowing their congregation to minister vicariously through them.

_____ 4. Pastors who equip others for ministry enable them to exercise their God-given gifts.

_____ 5. A pastor knows they are accomplishing their pastoral task as other believers use their spiritual gifts.

_____ 6. Christians who want to use their spiritual gifts must derive their power and authority from the staff leaders of the congregation.

_____ 7. A healthy church is one in which the pastor alone functions in their God-assigned ministry.

_____ 8. Laypersons are capable of and should be expected to render effective ministry to others while using their spiritual gifts.

_____ 9. God is the ultimate source of ministry empowerment.

_____ 10. An unhealthy pastor serves the church by this principle: If you want a job done right, do it yourself.

Further Reflection:
In what ways are you tempted to under-function in your church?

What tasks has the Lord called you to in a whisper?

CHAPTER 8

Impacting the World

Objectives

1. We will explore various aspects of community and global service.
2. We will assess what kinds of work the local church can do in its community.
3. We will commit to using our time and votes to create a more just society.

The following words of Jesus are recorded in John 15: "I am the vine; you are the branches. If a man remains in me and I in him, he will bear much fruit; apart from me you can do nothing. If anyone does not remain in me, he is like a branch that is thrown away and withers; such branches are picked up, thrown into the fire and burned. If you remain in me and my words remain in you, ask whatever you wish, and it will be given you. This is to my Father's glory, that you bear much fruit, showing yourselves to be my disciples" (vv 5–8).

As Christians reflect these concerns of Christ, we will endeavor not only to discover our spiritual gifts and share them with each other but also to discern how God has equipped us to make a difference in the world. We have significant opportunities to bear spiritual fruit as we engage in various forms of community service. Some of these activities require specific spiritual gifts to ensure success; however, several service opportunities may require love and time alone.

In *Churches That Make a Difference*, the authors identify four basic categories of social action: relief, individual development, community development, and structural change. Let us explore what each of these means.

Relief is analogous to giving a hungry person a fish. Relief ministry ensures the survival of needy people. Congregations that offer relief provide food, clothing, or shelter to people in urgent need.[1] Examples of relief ministries include food pantries, clothes closets, homeless shelters, family crisis hotlines, free immunizations, safe houses, vouchers for medicine, and programs that assist families to avoid having their utilities shut off because of non-payment.

The church I serve as pastor, the Metropolitan Church of God in Detroit, Michigan, has a relief ministry called Food 4 Families. Four times a year we turn the church parking lot into a drive-thru distribution center where we give away a week's supply of groceries to four hundred families in the community who have registered for the free food. In this food distribution, we do not discriminate based on income, number of family members, or religious preference.[2]

Individual development is like teaching a person how to fish and where to fish. Individual development helps to ensure someone else's independence. It empowers persons "to improve [their] physical, emotional, intellectual, relational, or social status."[3] Sider, Olson, and Unruh explain, "Individual development ministries may include credit counseling or debt management courses, job training and interview coaching, and health seminars."[4] Individual development may also include alcohol and drug addiction counseling, home owner seminars, GED tutoring, job training, interview training, budget counseling,

---

1. Sider, Olson, and Unruh, *Churches That Make a Difference*, 86.
2. To find out more about Food 4 Families, visit www.metropolitancog.org.
3. Sider, Olson, and Unruh, *Churches That Make a Difference*, 86.
4. Ibid.

parenting classes, divorce recovery classes, Overeaters Anonymous programs, and more.

An example is Financial Peace University, an individual development ministry offered by many churches across the United States. This ministry teaches persons within a community how to take control of their money, invest for their future, and give their tithes and offerings.[5]

Community development is analogous to providing the people of an area with the equipment they need to fish. Community development, like individual development, helps to ensure a sustainable way of life. It seeks to "renew the building blocks of a healthy community, such as housing, jobs, health care, and education."[6] Examples of community development include construction of affordable housing, daycare services, after-school programs, and a community gym. Congregations that engage in community development may also launch and maintain rehabilitation centers, legal aid clinics, small-business training, and grant-writing seminars.

First Presbyterian Church in Mount Holly, New Jersey, started a separate nonprofit ministry called Homes of Hope, Inc., for the purpose of community development. Birthed to address the issue of decaying homes and lack of affordable housing in the area surrounding First Presbyterian, this ministry buys, restores, and rents housing to lower-income families.[7]

Structural change would be like helping everyone in a community get fair access to the fish pond and making sure there are enough fish in the pond. Congregations involved in structural change work to transform unfair political, economic, environmental, or cultural institutions and systems. This is to say that they work to correct sinful structures in society. Structural change may take the form of lobbying against insurance redlining, standing in support of mass-transit systems in communities that lack it, and encouraging elected government officials to provide health care for those who cannot afford it on their own.[8]

---

5. To learn more about Financial Peace University, visit www.daveramsey.com.

6. Sider, Olson, and Unruh, *Churches That Make a Difference*, 86.

7. For more information on Homes of Hope, visit www.affordablehomesgroup.com/homesof-hope/index.htm.

8. Sider, Olson, and Unruh, *Churches That Make a Difference*, 86.

Churches that work to achieve structural change may also lobby to raise the minimum wage, acquire health coverage for low-income families, and fight for equal rights and pay for women in the workplace.

Fellowship Chapel, in Detroit, Michigan, birthed the Fannie Lou Hamer Political Action Committee. Registered with state and federal authorities, this political action committee (PAC) registers voters and canvases neighborhoods in an effort to support its endorsed candidates. According to its website, "the FLH-PAC, with an 85% success rate, has quickly become a major political force in Detroit, and our work still grows because we…believe commitment must bring action."[9]

In order for the church to combat the sinful structures of society, its members cannot fear or fail to be involved in the political system. The New Testament does not mention any direct political involvement by Christ, and some Christians believe this means they should abandon the modern political system altogether. However, a clear understanding of Jesus and the political climate of his day will give us a different perspective on the political involvement of individual Christians and the church as a whole.

Jesus was part of "an oppressed colony ruled by a totalitarian, imperialistic Roman dictatorship. He had no Roman political rights."[10] In his day, persons who had no legal power generally opted for one of three political stances, yet all three violated the values of the kingdom that Jesus was introducing.

One option was selected by the Herodians and Sadducees, who "collaborated with the oppressive Romans to protect and extend their privileged, unjust lives."[11] Obviously, this did not square with Jesus' teaching that his disciples will care for the needs of others.

A second option was the choice of the Essenes, who moved to the desert and formed "a separatist community, waiting passively for the coming of the Messiah."[12] Jesus never intended to withdraw from the problems of society, nor did he instruct his disciples to withdraw.

---

9. Fannie Lou Hamer Political Action Committee, "About Us," http://www.flhpac.org/index.php?id=1 (accessed December 5, 2012).

10. Ronald Sider, *Good News and Good Works*, 152.

11. Ibid.

12. Ibid.

A third political option was that of the revolutionary Zealots, who attempted to drive out the Roman oppressors through war.[13] The third option, however, would not allow Jesus to love his enemies as he taught his disciples to do.

Therefore, Jesus created his own option. Sider writes, "(He) summoned the entire society to change and then form a new community living at the heart of the society for all those ready to challenge the status quo."[14] Since Jesus was not afforded the opportunity that democratic governments provide, he was not directly involved in the political arena of his day; but this does not excuse his followers from being intimately involved in their political systems. Believers should allow the living Christ to use their hands, feet, mouths, and votes within the political system so that he can continue to heal personal and social sin.

We Christians must also grasp the fact that evangelism should be directed toward everyone, while social action should be primarily directed toward the interests of the vulnerable. Every human stands in need of a relationship with Christ and admission into the new community inaugurated by Christ. Evangelistic efforts must be geared to benefit everyone under the sun. While social action may have an effect on everyone, it should be directed toward empowering the disinherited.

Knowing who the church should focus on will help the church have a holistic ministry approach. In their book *Toward an Evangelical Public Policy*, Ron Sider and Diane Knippers provide a list of eleven at-risk groups that the church should endeavor to assist:

(1)   the poor, both those who are chronically unemployed and those who work for very low wages;

(2)   women, who often get paid less for similar work and are disproportionately the victims of mental abuse, social discrimination, and physical violence;

(3)   children, who must be protected from abandonment, childhood labor, forced military recruitment, gangs, and sexual abuse, while being provided an adequate education;

---

13. Ibid., 153.
14. Ibid.

(4) immigrants who cross cultural and national borders in search of better lives, especially those of lower socioeconomic status;

(5) refugees, who deal with similar struggles as immigrants combined with painful experiences from their homeland, which may leave them with few prospects to return to a normal way of life in their country of origin,

(6) the sick, who may experience pain, fear, abandonment, or rejection, and who may also have to deal with exorbitant health-care bills they cannot afford;

(7) persons with disabilities, who must be protected from rejection, mistreatment, and abandonment;

(8) the persecuted, who are oppressed because of their race, gender, ethnicity, or creed;

(9) minorities, who seem powerless because they are outnumbered and are often overlooked by justice;

(10) the addicted, who deal with debilitating enslavements to things such as drugs, alcohol, pornography, and gambling;

(11) prisoners, who face the loss of freedom, dignity, and respect, and need help to reintegrate themselves back into society after their sentences are over.[15]

The Lord took up the cause of the vulnerable and weak; so too should his followers. The body of Christ has a historic window of opportunity because of the current political climate, which allows government funding of faith-based organizations. This was evidenced by President George W. Bush's ongoing support of faith-based organizations. Moreover, "secular journalists, academics, and public policy experts have developed an amazing openness to an expanded role for faith-based organizations in overcoming poverty."[16] If the body of Christ in the United States does not seize this opportunity to shine its light through the combination of evangelism, relief activities, community development, and efforts to change our unjust social structures, the quality of life in this country will continue to decay.

---

15. Sider and Knippers, *Toward an Evangelical Public Policy*, 229–31.
16. Sider, Olson, and Unruh, *Churches That Make a Difference*, 12.

QUIZ 8
Gifts of the Spirit

Next to each statement, write *T* for true or *F* for false.

_____ 1. As Christians share their spiritual gifts with other Christians, they should also look for ways to serve outside of the Christian community.

_____ 2. It is unlikely that a person's spiritual gift can be used effectively outside the church.

_____ 3. Marginalized people need additional resources and opportunities to succeed.

_____ 4. Congregations should always choose to add more Bible studies instead of secular GED programs.

_____ 5. A Christian's material resources are always best used feeding and clothing the hungry and naked.

_____ 6. Christians should strive to ensure that people of their community have both Jesus and jobs.

_____ 7. Jesus would be pleased to see a congregation offer credit and debt management training, both to believers and unbelievers.

_____ 8. Since Jesus never voted, Christians should avoid politics and work for change outside of the political system.

_____ 9. Christians everywhere should be concerned about the just treatment of immigrants.

_____ 10. Congregations should not accept government funds allocated for faith-based organizations to address poverty.

Further Reflection:

What at-risk groups do you come in contact with on a daily basis?

How can you use your democratic rights to aid these individuals?

CHAPTER 9

Spiritual Gifts of 1 Corinthians 12

Objectives

1. We will review the thirteen spiritual gifts supplied in 1 Corinthians 12.

2. We will cherish the fact that there are innumerable spiritual gifts in the kingdom of God.

3. We build upon our existing knowledge of spiritual gifts.

A spiritual gift has been defined as "a special ability that God gives, according to his grace, to each member of the body of Christ to be used for the development of the kingdom."[1] No biblical text claims to have an exhaustive list of the gifts of the Spirit, but this lesson explores the biblical chapter that lists the most gifts.[2] The apostle Paul wrote the following in 1 Corinthians 12:7–11:

---

1. Schwarz, *3 Colors of Ministry*, 42. See chapter 3 for detailed discussion of definition.

2. 1 Corinthians 12 lists thirteen spiritual gifts; the complete text of 1 Corinthians 12 is available in Appendix A. Romans 12:6–8 has seven spiritual gifts: prophecy, service, teaching, encouraging, giving, leadership, and mercy. Ephesians 4:11 enumerates five spiritual gifts: apostles, prophets, evangelists, pastors, and teachers.

> Now to each one the manifestation of the Spirit is given for the common good. To one there is given through the Spirit the message of wisdom, to another the message of knowledge by means of the same Spirit, to another faith by the same Spirit, to another gifts of healing by that one Spirit, to another miraculous powers, to another prophecy, to another distinguishing between spirits, to another speaking in different kinds of tongues, and to still another the interpretation of tongues. All these are the work of one and the same Spirit, and he gives them to each one, just as he determines.

As Paul elaborates on what he has written in verse seven, he describes nine ways that the Spirit is manifested within the Christian community. Later in the chapter, Paul lists four additional spiritual gifts (v 28). Apparently, Paul's intent in 1 Corinthians 12 is not to offer an exhaustive list of spiritual gifts or "to identify the precise nature of the gifts."[3] Rather, he seems intent upon highlighting the diversity of ways in which the Spirit is manifested.

Message of Wisdom

The first manifestation listed in the passage is *the message of wisdom*. In light of 1 Corinthians 2:6–16, Paul understands true wisdom as the "recognition of the message of Christ crucified."[4] In a practical sense, those with the gift of wisdom are able to diagnose personal or congregational problems and offer solutions. Individuals in the church recognize the gift of wisdom in other believers and approach them for counseling, advice, and instruction, especially as it pertains to life-altering decisions.

An example of a believer graced with the gift of wisdom is Jerald January, the senior pastor of Vernon Park Church of God in Chicago, Illinois. January serves the body of Christ as a church consultant. He works with the pastors and leaders of local congregations to help them understand their context, enhance their ministry, make godly decisions in light of their strengths, weaknesses, opportunities, and threats.

---

3. Garland, *1 Corinthians*, 580.
4. Ibid., 592.

A person with the gift of wisdom is also empowered by the Holy Spirit to counsel, assist in conflict resolution, serve as a member of the local church's governing board, and engage in a wide variety of other ministries that need the gift of wisdom.

Message of Knowledge.

The second manifestation listed is the *message of knowledge*. Most Bible scholars believe that Paul is alluding to the ability to gain information supernaturally.[5] When the Sprit is manifested through this gift, a believer becomes aware of information that only the Spirit could have supplied.[6] A Christian who possesses this gift may often find others asking, "There's no way you could've known that—how in the world did you find out?"

A missionary from Baltimore, Maryland, recounted to me an experience that demonstrated the use of the gift of knowledge. At the end of her assignment in a foreign country, she told the others in her group that she felt impressed by the Holy Spirit to leave three days early. The group followed her counsel and avoided being stranded in the country due to a civil uprising that occurred the day they had been scheduled to leave. Members of the body of Christ with the message of knowledge may lead in seminar preparation, long-term planning, Bible studies, creative evangelistic efforts, and a host of other ministries that require this gift.[7]

Faith

Faith is the third manifestation Paul includes in the list. Similar to the gift of knowledge, faith involves the supernatural. Every believer has been empowered by the Spirit with the faith necessary for salvation; however, here Paul is referring to a supernatural manifestation of faith that is "able to move mountains" (see 1 Cor 13:2). Gordon Fee appropriately says that a spiritual gift of faith is the "supernatural

---

5. Garland, *1 Corinthians*, 592.

6. Schwarz, *3 Colors of Ministry*, 112.

7. Ibid., 107.

conviction that God will reveal his power or mercy in a special way in a specific instance."[8]

Acts 27:13–44 provides a good illustration of the gift of faith. Although Paul and his captors were caught in the middle of a terrible storm at sea, Paul declared the message the Lord gave him that none of their lives would be lost—and so it was. Members with this spiritual gift might serve as prayer group leaders, church council members, congregational long-term planners, church planters, or in an assortment of other ministries that require above-average faith.[9]

Healing

The fourth manifestation is the gift of *healing*. God uses individuals graced with this gift to facilitate the physical healing of others. Note that a spiritual gift enables a believer to repeatedly express a special ability given by God. If a Christian, therefore, "is granted the *charisma* to heal one particular individual of one particular disease at one time, that Christian should not presume to think the *gift* of healing has been bestowed on him or her, prompting the founding of a healing ministry."[10]

Peter demonstrated the spiritual gift of healing on a number of occasions in the book of Acts. In Acts 3:1–10, for example, Peter healed a lame beggar. Acts 5:15 states that people brought their sick onto the streets in the earnest hope that Peter's shadow falling on them would provide healing. (Note that the Scripture text does not specifically state that Peter's shadow healed the sick; however, the context suggests that he was known for this ability.) Peter also healed a paralyzed man in Lydda and raised a dead woman to life in Joppa (Acts 9:32–42). Believers who have the gift of healing might serve in prayer groups and visitation teams, conduct healing services, or engage in other ministries that require such a gift.[11]

---

8. Fee, *First Epistle to the Corinthians*, 593.

9. Schwarz, *3 Colors of Ministry*, 127.

10. Garland, *1 Corinthians*, 582. *Charisma* is the Greek word commonly translated as *grace* or *gift*.

11. Schwarz, *3 Colors of Ministry*, 129.

Miraculous Powers

Fifth, Paul lists the manifestation of *miraculous powers*. This broad category includes all supernatural activities not associated with physical healing. In essence, "it covers a broad range of supernatural events that ordinary parlance would call miraculous."[12] The application of the gift of miraculous powers is often linked to the release of God's people or to evangelistic efforts to save the lost.

We find notable examples of this empowerment in the book of Exodus, which describes how Moses turned his staff into a snake, unleashed plagues upon Israel, and parted the Red Sea. A New Testament person who exercised this gift was Philip, during his ministry in Samaria. Acts 8:5–7 states, "Philip went down to a city in Samaria and proclaimed the Messiah there. When the crowds heard Philip and saw the signs he performed, they all paid close attention to what he said. For with shrieks, impure spirits came out of many, and many who were paralyzed or lame were healed" (NIV). Persons graced with this gift might be well-suited to engagement in foreign missions, revivals, spiritual warfare, evangelism, and other ministries that benefit from the demonstration of miraculous powers.

Prophecy

The sixth manifestation listed is *prophecy*. Paul and other biblical writers understood that a prophet is a person who speaks to the Lord's people under the inspiration of the Holy Spirit. Prophets can be described as "those who have been assaulted by, and are now obsessed with, the truth of God. Prophets are those who have unusual gifts for discernment into the purposes of God and who are unusually bold in bringing those purposes to speech."[13] In addition to having a passion for truth, believers gifted with prophecy also have a thirst for individual and communal righteousness. They are more concerned with truth, justice, and righteousness than being politically correct. Thus, the gift of prophecy gives Christians the boldness and confidence they need to speak truth to power.

---

12. Fee, *First Epistle to the Corinthians*, 595.
13. Willimon, *Proclamation and Theology*, 22.

The messages Old Testament prophets delivered on the Lord's behalf were often declarations of salvation and words of judgment. The prophet Joel stands as an example. When the people of God faced a natural disaster that consisted of an insect invasion, Joel boldly declared the Lord sent this punishment because of the people's sin. He writes,

> The LORD is at the head of the column.
> He leads them with a shout.
> This is his mighty army,
> and they follow his orders.
> The day of the LORD is an awesome, terrible thing.
> Who can possibly survive?
> That is why the LORD says,
> "Turn to me now, while there is time.
> Give me your hearts.
> Come with fasting, weeping, and mourning.
> Don't tear your clothing in your grief,
> but tear your hearts instead."
> Return to the LORD your God,
> for he is merciful and compassionate,
> slow to get angry and filled with unfailing love.
> He is eager to relent and not punish.
> Who knows? Perhaps he will give you a reprieve,
> sending you a blessing instead of this curse.
> Perhaps you will be able to offer grain and wine
> to the LORD your God as before.
> (Joel 2:11–14 NLT)

The messages of Old Testament prophets often had futuristic elements; however, the act of predicting is never the most crucial role of a prophet. The New Testament offers additional insight on the purpose of prophecy in 1 Corinthians 14:3, "The one who prophesies speaks to people for their strengthening, encouraging and comfort" (NIV).

When contemporary Christians refer to the gift of preaching, they usually mean the gift of prophecy. It is important, however, to grasp the fact that not everyone graced with the gift of prophecy preaches, but the most effective preachers have the spiritual gift of prophecy. Consequently, the gift of prophecy is demonstrated on a weekly basis in many local congregations. People gifted with prophecy are also suited to serve as national church leaders, teachers, evangelists, authors, counselors, and in other ministries that require this spiritual gift.

Distinguishing Between Spirits/Discernment

Seventh, Paul lists the gift of *distinguishing between spirits*, more commonly called the gift of discernment. Those graced with discernment are enabled to differentiate between "what is truly of the Spirit of God and what comes from other spirits."[14] This gift empowers an individual to distinguish between right and wrong, truth and error. For instance, the gift of discernment is used to properly judge and validate prophecies. Moreover, the ability to distinguish between spirits is often a critical companion gift to prophecy. The idea that the spiritual gifts of prophecy and discernment are connected is suggested by Paul's comment in 1 Corinthians 14, "Two or three prophets should speak, and the others should weigh carefully what is said" (14:29). Christians graced with discernment are equipped to serve in a congregation's church council, deliverance ministry, trustee board, as well as in other areas that need this gift.

Speaking in Different Kinds of Tongues.

The eighth manifestation listed is *speaking in different kinds of tongues*. This controversial gift threatened to divide the Corinthian church. Some members in the Corinthian church bragged about having the gift of tongues, and some improperly believed they were more spiritual than those who had not been graced with the gift of tongues. The Corinthian preference for this manifestation served as the catalyst for Paul's entire argument that spans three chapters of his first epistle to the Corinthians (chapters 12–14).

---

14. Fee, *First Epistle to the Corinthians*, 595.

While there is a good deal of disagreement among biblical scholars about the exact nature of the spiritual gift of speaking in different kinds of tongues, most believe that Paul here refers to a language unintelligible to the speaker and most of his or her hearers. While acknowledging the disagreement of sincere Bible students at this point, I believe it is important to examine what Scripture says about two particular forms of this spiritual gift.

First, a person graced with this gift may be supernaturally enabled to utter prophecy in a known human language which that person has never studied, although it is clearly understood by those who do speak it. For example, a person who never learned French can be empowered by the Holy Spirit to share the gospel in French to a person from France. This is clearly what took place on the day of Pentecost as recorded in Acts 2:1–13.

Second, a person graced with this gift may be moved by the Holy Spirit to prophesy publicly using an ecstatic utterance that neither the speaker nor the hearers would normally understand. In order for such an ecstatic utterance to edify the church (proof that it is a genuine spiritual gift), the message must be interpreted, according to 1 Corinthians 14:5. I witnessed an occurrence of this second form of the gift during a camp meeting of the National Association of the Church of God in West Middlesex, Pennsylvania, when a speaker at the podium began to speak in ecstatic utterance. He then proceeded to interpret the message, putting it into English and using hand gestures that mimicked the ones he used while speaking in tongues.[15]

Persons graced with either form of this gift are equipped to evangelize unbelievers and strengthen, encourage, challenge, or comfort believers. Unfortunately, some religious bodies continue to debate the validity of this gift. In light of this fact, believers should be aware of a few pertinent points of information about this gift.

First, Christians must understand and accept the fact that the Holy Spirit may chose to grace present-day believers with a supernatural ability to speak in different languages. "Paul would tell us that just as

---

15. The instruction of 1 Corinthians 14:13 makes it clear that a person gifted with speaking in different kinds of tongues may also be spiritually gifted with the interpretation of tongues.

'charismania,' an overemphasis on prophecy or tongues, is not healthy, neither is 'charisphobia,' the anathematizing of all such gifts."[16]

Second, we must not confuse the gift of tongues, which God gives for the edification of the church, with personal prayer or praise language, which is not for that purpose. Paul appears to refer to such a language in 1 Corinthians 14:2–19. He says in part,

> For anyone who speaks in a tongue does not speak to people but to God. Indeed, no one understands them; they utter mysteries by the Spirit…Anyone who speaks in a tongue edifies themselves, but the one who prophesies edifies the church. (vv 2, 4 NIV)

Again, since this kind of personal utterance does not edify others, it cannot be considered a spiritual gift like the others described in this book.[17]

Third, while personal prayer language cannot be labeled as a spiritual gift, the practice of praying in tongues privately as a form of intercession for others should to be classified as a spiritual gift. I have had conversations with a variety of believers who testify that they regularly intercede for others while praying in an unknown language. They tend to know who they are praying for, but do not always know what they are praying for. Christians who are able to authentically intercede for others by praying in tongues can only do so because they have been graced by the Holy Spirit with this unique ability. Due to the private nature of this form of gifted praying, it does not require interpretation the way it would if it were uttered publicly.

Fourth, speaking in different kinds of tongues does not prove that someone has the Holy Spirit's infilling.[18] Galatians 5:22–23 lists the fruit of the Spirit (clear evidence of the Holy Spirit's infilling) as "love, joy, peace, forbearance, kindness, goodness, faithfulness, gentleness and self-control" (NIV).

---

16. Witherington, *Conflict and Community in Corinth*, 263.

17. Christians who have the ability to pray or praise in tongues often do so to make incomprehensible personal petition or to please God. Although public expression of this ability is prohibited, it is acceptable when done privately.

18. People who believe this appear to assume that a biblical *description* is a biblical *prescription*.

Finally, believers should grasp the fact that their congregation will have a person graced with the gift of tongues only if the Holy Spirit wills it to be that way. The Holy Spirit gives every local congregation all the spiritual gifts it needs across a variety of persons. It seems reasonable to conclude that if no one in a congregation exercises the gift of tongues (of either type), the Lord has sovereignly determined that they do not need this gift to properly function.

Interpretation of Tongues

The ninth manifestation listed is the *interpretation of tongues*. Interpretation is the required companion of the gift of speaking in different kinds of tongues when done publicly because of the unintelligible nature of the latter. According to Paul's line of reasoning, the interpretation of tongues is just as inspired by the Spirit as the other gifts he has listed. A person with the gift of interpretation may be empowered to translate a known human language they have never studied so other people can understand a message sent from God in the form of that foreign language. (Note that the Greek word here translated as *interpretation* literally means "to put in words."[19]) On the other hand, a person with the spiritual gift of interpretation may be able to take a message declared in an ecstatic utterance and put it into intelligible words so that anyone present can understand what has been said by the person so speaking. This means that believers graced with the interpretation of tongues are able to legitimize the public expression of an ecstatic utterance if they adhere to biblical guidelines for such activity. The biblical guidelines are expressed in 1 Corinthians 14:27–28,

> If anyone speaks in a tongue, two—or at the most three— should speak, one at a time, and someone must interpret. If there is no interpreter, the speaker should keep quiet in the church and speak to himself and to God."

---

19. Fee, *First Epistle to the Corinthians*, 598.

Believers graced with the spiritual gift of discernment may be able to further validate the legitimacy of a message spoken ecstatically and then interpreted by someone so gifted. [20]

Besides the spiritual gifts already listed, Paul enumerates four more manifestations in verse 28: apostles, teachers, helps, and administration.

Apostle

The tenth manifestation is often referred to as the spiritual gift of *apostle*.[21] In a strict historical sense, there were twelve individuals who held the title or office of apostle, the eleven original disciples and Matthias, who replaced Judas. These individuals are classified as apostles because they:

- were with Jesus during his earthly ministry from his baptism to ascension;

- witnessed the resurrection of Jesus Christ;

- performed signs and wonders; and

- provided the foundational teachings of the church (Acts 1:21–22 and 2:42–43).

According to these criteria, we must say that the title and office of apostle passed away forever with the deaths of the Twelve. However, the Bible does refer to Barnabas, James, Silas, Timothy, and Paul as apostles even though they do not meet all the restrictive criteria

---

20. For additional guidelines for local congregations, see Callen, *Following Our Lord*, 104–5.

21. The uncertainty and disagreement regarding apostleship is second only to the spiritual gift of speaking in different kinds of tongues. In addition to the view presented here, others argue that (1) the spiritual gift of apostle is no longer given by the Holy Spirit; (2) it is synonymous with the gift of missionary; and (3) it refers to a church planter. In the midst of such divergent understandings, Christians can take comfort in knowing the Holy Spirit will empower certain believers to foster cooperative Christian efforts, establish new local congregations, and evangelize and minister to foreigners, whether or not they properly identify or define his method of equipping.

mentioned earlier.[22] In what sense were these individuals apostles? And how might a modern-day Christian have the spiritual gift of apostle?

According to biblical scholar Gordon Fee, "For Paul [apostle] is both a 'functional' and positional/official' term."[23] Consequently, the ministry and function of these other apostles suggest that we should have a broader understanding of the spiritual gift of apostle. Individuals graced with the gift of apostle "have a special spiritual power to get groups of persons moving on the same track towards common goals."[24] A believer graced with this gift has the necessary power, influence, charisma, and respect to cause local congregations to unify and work cooperatively with one another. They have the ability to help pastors and other leaders see and pursue accomplishments that they could only achieve while working together. Persons exercising this gift also tend to be greatly involved in spreading the influence of the kingdom of God though church planting.[25]

Bill Jones, state pastor of the Church of God in Michigan, is an example of one graced with the gift of apostle. He works strategically and practically to bring the churches associated with the Church of God in Michigan together to make a substantial and unified impact for the kingdom of God. Jones also makes himself available to shepherd and mentor the pastors of the state. The power of his spiritual gift enables him to carry out these tasks despite the lack of any ecclesiastical structure that requires the churches and pastors in Michigan to obey his recommendations. Believers graced with this spiritual gift are also empowered to serve as denominational leaders; national, state, or regional overseers; chief development officers; leaders of local ministerial assemblies; as well as other ministries that require the gift of apostle.

---

22. See Acts 14:14; Galatians 1:19; 1 Thessalonians 1:1; 2:6; and Romans 1:1. Andronicus and Junia are described as "outstanding among the apostles" in Romans 16:7. These two either stood as apostles or were esteemed by those who were apostles.

23. Fee, *First Epistle to the Corinthians*, 620.

24. Bryant, *Rediscovering Our Spiritual Gifts*, 64.

25. Christians today are well advised to avoid using the title of apostle even though some believers are graced to exercise the spiritual gift of apostle since the title and office no longer exist and in deference to those the Bible specifically refers to as apostles. As with other spiritual gifts, a believer does not need to use a title or name of a gift in order to use it effectively.

Teaching

The eleventh manifestation listed in 1 Corinthians 12 is *teaching*. Members of the body of Christ who have the gift of teaching long to know and communicate the truth, so they are driven by a desire to clarify truth to others. They are able to take complicated realities and present them in ways that others will understand. Persons graced with this gift "can bring out the deep things of God that have been hidden and delight to see 'light bulbs' go off in others."[26] While a believer with the gift of knowledge understands things supernaturally, a person gifted to teach has the ability to search for biblical truth that has already been revealed and successfully impart that truth to others. Leslie Flynn makes this significant point in her book *19 Gifts of the Spirit*:

> It is possible for a Christian to have a talent for teaching, but not have the spiritual gift of teaching…He would be quite capable of imparting considerable information and knowledge of facts about the lessons of his class but his teaching would lack the power to bless, to advance his students spiritually.[27]

While secular teachers will not automatically make the best Sunday school and Bible study teachers, those who have the natural ability to teach may also be graced by God to teach.

The late Gilbert W. Stafford, former director of the Doctor of Ministry Program at Anderson University School of Theology, serves as an example of one graced with the gift of teaching. He taught systematic theology in the seminary for years, helping thousands of seminarians to build firm theological foundations. Many of Stafford's students have gone on to pastor, minister as professors, and write books. Christians graced to teach may serve as senior or associate pastors, or lead small groups, seminars, Bible studies, training events, and a host of other ministries that require this gift.

---

26. Wollensack, *Called to Be, Called to Do*, 59.
27. Flynn, *19 Gifts of the Spirit*, 85.

Helps

The twelfth manifestation listed is *helps*. This refers to an unusual ability to meet the material needs of other church members—and perhaps their spiritual needs as well. The spiritual gift of helps frees other members to exercise their spiritual gifts. Christians graced with the gift of helps are individuals that everyone can count on for innumerable forms of assistance—from setting up chairs to visiting the sick to transporting seniors on Sunday mornings—whether or not the persons so gifted have official titles or assignments for these ministries. Those who possess this gift will approach other believers and say, "Let me do this so you can focus on other things." Members graced with the gift of helps often choose to minister in private ways. They are motivated to complete their tasks and are ready to perform those tasks themselves instead of delegating them to others.

People with the gift of helps frequently find themselves being helpful to other members of the body of Christ wherever they go. Terry Reggie Keys, a former member of the Metropolitan Church of God in Detroit, Michigan, was a true example of one who possessed the gift of helps. He served in a variety of official capacities within the congregation, including roles on the trustee board, youth advisory team, and usher board. Yet his ministry reached far beyond his official roles. Keys was always able and willing to assume a task that suddenly needed to be carried out. He would cheerfully help other members carry out their responsibilities, even if someone else had failed to plan properly. Keys has now relocated and has become a blessing to members of True Vision Church in San Antonio, Texas. Those graced with the gift of helps might make telephone calls, work as youth chaperones, perform secretarial or custodial work, or assume a host of other duties—whatever the Body needs.

Administration

The thirteenth manifestation listed is the spiritual gift of *administration* or organizing. A person with this gift guides and counsels the community of faith so that it moves in the direction that its leadership discerns it needs to go.[28] This concept is well-described by the following from Schwarz: "The captain makes the basic decisions regarding the route of the ship [or church] and the helmsman [or administrator/organizer] guides the ship safely to her intended course."[29] Christians with this gift pay attention to logistical details; they anticipate the congregation's ministry needs and potential problems with remarkable accuracy. They excel in the proper management of people, time, and resources and do not shy away from asking tough questions about procedure. They naturally follow a familiar exhortation by the late Alex F. Wallace, "Get a plan and work your plan."[30]

Patricia Arnold, a member of Center of Hope Church in Inglewood, California, well embodies the gift of administration. Arnold has served for several years as the registrar for the National Inspiration Youth Convention. Her giftedness has allowed her to contribute significantly in the contract negotiations with hotels that house the youth convention. Her attention to detail, ability to establish functional systems, and skill at successful management of her staff and budget has allowed thousands of youth and adults from across the United States to register and attend these annual conventions. Christians with this gift are equipped to oversee other ministries, manage church growth planning, organize church events, administer finances, conduct evangelistic campaigns, coordinate technological media, and engage in a host of other functions that need the gift of administration.

While the thirteen spiritual gifts listed in 1 Corinthians 12 contribute significantly to the edification of the church, other gifts exist beyond this list. Your growing knowledge of spiritual gifts will increase the likelihood that you will discover the gift or gifts you possess.

---

28. Fee, *First Epistle to the Corinthians*, 622.

29. Schwarz, *3 Colors of Ministry*, 110.

30. Alex F. Wallace (associate minister of New Faith Ministries, Indianapolis, Indiana), sermon, October 20, 2002.

QUIZ 9
Gifts of the Spirit

Next to each statement, write *T* for true or *F* for false.

_____ 1. Scripture does not provide an exhaustive list of spiritual gifts.

_____ 2. The gift of wisdom enables a believer to diagnose congregational problems and prescribe effective solutions for them.

_____ 3. The gift of knowledge can be obtained through years of academic study.

_____ 4. The spiritual gift of faith is required for salvation.

_____ 5. Every congregation should have a healing ministry.

_____ 6. Biblically, effective preachers are also prophets.

_____ 7. A person who uses the gift of tongues speaks a language unknown to himself or herself and his or her hearers.

_____ 8. The gift of tongues is always accompanied by the gift of interpretation when used appropriately.

_____ 9. An experienced schoolteacher surely has the spiritual gift of teaching.

_____ 10. A person with the gift of administration is best equipped to distinguish between legitimate and illegitimate preaching.

Further Reflection:
Do you believe you have any of the spiritual gifts mentioned?

If so, which ones?

CHAPTER 10

Spiritual Gifts Related to Practical Needs

Objectives

1. We will examine a variety of spiritual gifts not identified in the Bible.

2. We will consider whether we have any of these spiritual gifts.

3. We will consider the spiritual gifts of other members of the church.

In this lesson, we will examine several spiritual gifts not listed in 1 Corinthians 12. As this exploration ensues, it is important to remember two things: (1) A spiritual gift is any "special ability that God gives, according to his grace, to each member of the body of Christ to be used for the development of the kingdom."[1] (2) Whereas the fruit of the Spirit are listed in Galatians 5:22–23, no biblical text claims to have an exhaustive list of the gifts of the Spirit. All of the spiritual gifts we are about to describe have the five characteristics that make up our

---

1. Schwarz, *3 Colors of Ministry*, 42.

definition of a spiritual gift,[2] yet not all of them are specifically listed in Scripture.[3]

In this lesson, we are going to survey several spiritual gifts that relate to practical needs. These include giving, encouraging, hospitality, mercy, and service.

Giving

The spiritual gift of *giving* is mentioned in Romans 12:8. Every Christian has a responsibility to contribute 10 percent of their income, along with what they decide to give as an offering, to their local congregation, so no one needs a special spiritual gift to do this. However, some believers are spiritually gifted to joyously and generously give well beyond what God requires. Persons who possess the gift of giving may regularly donate something extra to a local congregation, Christian causes, or to individuals who stand in need.

Members of the church graced with this gift freely give without expecting anything in return; "they simply become channels for the Lord to use for the distribution of His resources, for they are convinced everything belongs to Him."[4] Members of the congregation who donate beyond what is required with the object of obtaining social power or status do not really have the gift of giving. The book of Acts documents a positive example of a person with this gift:

> There was a Levite, a native of Cyprus, Joseph, to whom the apostles gave the name Barnabas (which means "son of encouragement"). He sold a field that belonged to him, then brought the money, and laid it at the apostles' feet. (Acts 4:36–38 NRSV)

Immediately following this account, we read about a married couple named Ananias and Sapphira who donated partial proceeds from their

---

2. See chapter 3 for discussion of the five elements of the spiritual gift definition.

3. While I use the term *spiritual gift* for all manifestations that fall within our definition of a spiritual gift, some may prefer to apply the term *spiritual empowerment* to such manifestations not specifically mentioned in the Bible. Also note that I make no attempt to describe every possible spiritual gift in this book. After all, the Holy Spirit in his sovereignty may choose to confer new spiritual gifts upon the church as he deems necessary.

4. Fortune, *Discover Your God-Given Gifts*, 139.

land sale, but claimed that they were donating all the proceeds (Acts 5:1-11). This couple may have coveted the accolades given to Barnabas; clearly, they were not spiritually gifted to give as Barnabas was.

It is important to note that the spiritual gift of giving is not contingent upon a person's wealth. The apostle Paul made this point in his next letter to the church in Corinth with regard to the Christians in Macedonia:

> We want you to know, brothers and sisters, about the grace of God that has been granted to the churches of Macedonia; for during a severe ordeal of affliction, their abundant joy and their extreme poverty have overflowed in a wealth of generosity on their part. For, as I can testify, they voluntarily gave according to their means, and even beyond their means, begging us earnestly for the privilege of sharing in this ministry to the saints. (2 Cor 8:1–4 NIV)

Christians with low or mid-level incomes who have been graced with the gift of giving may regularly give far more than 10 percent of their earnings for the work of the kingdom. My mother, the late Rita Joyce Williams, was graced with the spiritual gift of giving. Despite living on a limited income, she would frequently take food from her cabinets and give it to believers and nonbelievers who had less than she had. She shared her meager finances with others whom she saw were in need. Members with the gift of giving may serve well as project sponsors, treasurers, financial advisers for local congregations, financial supporters of college students and senior citizens, and in a variety of other areas.

Encouragement/Exhortation

The gift of *encouragement* (also known as the gift of exhortation) is listed in Romans 12:8. All Christians have the responsibility to encourage and uplift one another, as the apostle Paul wrote to the Thessalonians:

> For God has destined us not for wrath but for obtaining salvation through our Lord Jesus Christ, who died for us, so that whether we are awake or asleep we may live with him. Therefore encourage one another and build up each other, as indeed you are doing. (1 Thess 5:9–11 NIV)

However, members of the body of Christ with the spiritual gift of encouragement can uplift, support, and motivate others with greater frequency and success. While a person gifted to teach is primarily concerned with what other Christians know, one endowed to encourage is chiefly concerned with what other believers feel.

Persons with the gift of encouragement use it in at least three ways. First, they assist other Christians who battle depression, defeat, and despair by sharing Scripture, insight, and perspective. Encouragers tend to see the glass half-full and will remind the people of God of the promises of God. They will look at a congregation's most troublesome circumstances and ask, "If God is for us, who is against us?" (Rom 8:31b NIV). They remind other believers that their faith is an antidote for whatever troubles come their way. When other members of the body of Christ find themselves in a valley situation, people with the gift of encouragement let them know that God can bring them out of the valley. They instinctively know what words to use (and when to be silent) to lend support to those experiencing difficult times.

Second, people with this gift motivate other Christians to serve or continue to serve fellow believers by using their spiritual gifts. While all members of the church may invite each other to serve in the kingdom by using their talents and spiritual gifts, encouragers demonstrate their giftedness by their results: They actually move others to serve! Throughout history, countless Christian servants would have given up their ministry had it not been for the words, hugs, and attention of those graced with the gift of encouragement. These people gave them the resolve to keep going. A friend confided to me how there were occasions when she questioned her ministry to her local congregation and wanted to give up. She told me that if it had not been for one of our church's encouragers, she would have given up and resigned from her position. From time to time, this person would approach her and say how much she blessed the congregation, even though she seemed unaware of my friend's struggles.

Third, the gift of encouragement enables certain people to challenge other believers to grow in their relationship with Christ. They can inspire others to develop greater spiritual maturity. People with the gift of encouragement are ideally suited to serve as ushers, greeters, visitation team members, youth leaders, clergy appreciation committee members, and prison chaplains. Many other positions are best filled by someone with this gift to uplift, support, and motivate others.

Hospitality

A person with the spiritual gift of *hospitality* "loves and is comfortable not only when entertaining friends or relatives, but particularly when welcoming strangers."[5] Persons graced with hospitality are at the forefront of the church when fellowship and unity are needed. Churches that have a family atmosphere rely on members graced with the gift of hospitality. These folks enjoy planning social events for the church, such as potlucks, bowl-a-thons, and chili cook-offs. They joyfully take care of the details necessary for everyone to have a good time before and during these events. Christians with the gift of hospitality have an inner drive to make outsiders feel welcome. In fact, they are able to make newcomers feel like they have been a part of the congregation for years. When Christians relocate to a new community from far distances, they can benefit from the time and attention of church members who hold this gift. Servants with the gift of hospitality often exercise it by inviting individuals and their families to their homes for meals, and they tend to be happier when they have other people around them.

A striking picture of Abraham's hospitality can be found in Genesis 18:1–8:

The LORD appeared to Abraham by the oaks of Mamre, as he sat at the entrance of his tent in the heat of the day. He looked

---

5. Shumate and Hayes, *Discover Your Gifts*, 66.

up and saw three men standing near him. When he saw them, he ran from the tent entrance to meet them, and bowed down to the ground. He said, "My lord, if I find favor with you, do not pass by your servant. Let a little water be brought, and wash your feet, and rest yourselves under the tree. Let me bring a little bread, that you may refresh yourselves, and after that you may pass on—since you have come to your servant." So they said, "Do as you have said." And Abraham hastened into the tent to Sarah, and said, "Make ready quickly three measures of choice flour, knead it, and make cakes." Abraham ran to the herd, and took a calf, tender and good, and gave it to the servant, who hastened to prepare it. Then he took curds and milk and the calf that he had prepared, and set it before them; and he stood by them under the tree while they ate. (NRSV)

A congregation benefits when its members graced with hospitality call first-time visitors, invite them to return, and encourage first-time visitors to connect with them when they do return. Other ways in which people graced with this gift may serve include small-group facilitators, church greeters, ushers, food pantry volunteers, and leading assimilation efforts.

Mercy

The gift of *mercy* is also referenced in Romans 12:8. Christians with the gift of mercy tend to reach out to marginalized individuals. They offer loving and empathetic words, and strive to physically help those who are in need. In a real sense, "The more opportunity they have to give love, the more joyful and fulfilled they are."[6] When they were young, they may have been the sort "who brought home the lost dogs and the stray cats. They also brought home the lonely kids no one else cared for and were very noncritical."[7] Believers who have the gift of mercy illustrate the caring heart of God with their strong desire to bring comfort and healing. Filled with compassion, they readily aid

---

6. Fortune, *Discover You God-Given Gifts*, 182.

7. Ibid., 183.

those who suffer by bearing a degree of the person's burden themselves. Persons graced with this gift have such a heart for hurting people that they will assist individuals who are suffering the consequences of their own sin or bad decisions. Intrinsically nonjudgmental, persons with the gift of mercy will seldom say, "You made your bed; now lay in it!" Instead, they are motivated by the belief that "there, but for the grace of God, go I."[8]

A man graced with the gift of mercy appears in Jesus' parable of the Good Samaritan (see Luke 10:25–37). While a priest and Levite passed by a man who had been robbed and left for dead on a road, a Samaritan man came to his aid. The Samaritan had pity on the man, attended his wounds, paid for his lodging expenses, and made financial arrangements with the innkeeper to ensure any additional needs the man had would be addressed. A Christian graced with this gift is equipped to minister on crisis phone lines, counsel, intercede in prayer, minister to single parents, children of single parents, and prisoners, as well as other ministries that require extraordinary mercy.

Service

The spiritual gift of *service* permits members of the Body to notice, correctly assess, and take care of needs. This manifestation of the Spirit is referenced in Romans 12:7. Believers with the gift of service are inclined to see necessities and problems that other church members are unaware of; therefore; they tend to do things that would otherwise go undone. While a Christian with the gift of helps will focus on freeing other believers so they can have more time to use their own spiritual gifts, someone with the gift of service focuses on doing work simply because it needs be done. Unconcerned with public recognition, these people are willing to serve publically or privately. They are gifted to participate in a wide range of activities; no task is too big or small. Servers' attention to detail and sense of satisfaction when the task is complete is reason enough for them to invest long hours in service

---

8. First attributed to sixteenth-century English reformer John Bradford. "The Phrase Finder," http://www.phrases.org.uk/meanings/there-but-for-the-grace-of-god.html (accessed January 23, 2013).

projects. It's common for them to continue working well after others have gone home, despite being physically tired.

Andrea Johnson, a member of Covenant Faith Church of God in Chicago, Illinois, is a fine example of a Christian graced with the gift of service. I witnessed her work tirelessly behind the scenes at the National Association of the Church of God's In-Service Training Institute (I.S.T.I) even though she did not have an official title or responsibilities. From taking pictures to designing the souvenir booklet to organizing the week's Fun Night, Johnson continually found ways to serve. By the end of the week, many of the attendees affectionately referred to her as "Sister Support." In a conversation, Johnson shared, "I am one who likes to serve in some way, however I can. It would have felt wrong not to do something at ISTI. I get restless if I am not doing something and trying to take things up a notch."[9] She further expressed the attitude of service by saying, "I see a need and want to meet it or help others meet the need." Over the last eight years, Johnson has made a substantial impact on the congregational life at Covenant Faith. Combining her spiritual gifts of administration and service, Johnson established an administrative structure for the Young Adult Choir, renovated the Sunday school program that led to increased enrollment, redesigned the children's and nursery ministry, and enhanced the offering of ministries that were part of the church's Board of Christian Education.

Saints with this spiritual gift are capable of implementing new or reconfiguring current ministries. They do custodial work, cook, host church guests, move tables and chairs, serve as ushers, stewards, or church council members, along with a host of other responsibilities that require the gift of service.

---

9. Andrea Johnson (member of Covenant Faith Church of God), interview with the author, January 28, 2013.

QUIZ 10
Gifts of the Spirit

Next to each statement, write *T* for true or *F* for false.

_____ 1. The spiritual gift of giving is required for Christians to tithe consistently.

_____ 2. Christians with the gift of giving normally give in the belief that they will be financially rewarded for the seeds they plant in the ministry.

_____ 3. The gift of hospitality enables Christians to successfully cause strangers and newcomers to feel cherished.

_____ 4. If person has the gift of hospitality, they should automatically join the local usher board or greeters ministry.

_____ 5. The gift of mercy allows people to be taken advantage of without retaliating.

_____ 6. Believers who have the gift of mercy reflect the compassion of God.

_____ 7. A member of the church who invites half the church to their house to watch the Super Bowl every year probably has the gift of hospitality.

_____ 8. If a task does not promise fame or fortune, a person gifted for service is not likely to take the job.

_____ 9. Believers with the gift of encouragement may inspire other Christians to cling to their faith during tough times.

_____ 10. Members of the Body who possess the gift of service are equipped to serve in a wide range of ministries.

Further Reflection:
Which spiritual gifts mentioned do you believe you have, if any?

As you examined the details of a particular gift, did a specific member of your church come to mind? Within the next week, share your thoughts with them.

Spiritual Gifts Related to Sharing the Gospel, Leadership, and Spiritual Unleashing

Objectives

1. We will examine additional spiritual gifts.
2. We will assess whether we have any of these spiritual gifts.
3. We will consider whether other members of our church have these gifts.

In this chapter, we continue to explore the spiritual gifts that are not listed in 1 Corinthians 12. Generally speaking, this chapter will consider gifts related to sharing the gospel, leadership, and spiritual unleashing. The gift related to sharing the gospel is called *evangelism*. Spiritual manifestations related to leadership include *counseling, leadership*, and *pastoring*. The gift that relates to supernatural unleashing is called the gift of *deliverance*.

Evangelism

The spiritual gift of *evangelism* is mentioned in Ephesians 4:11. Evangelism is defined as "the communication of the good news of Jesus Christ—that He died for our sins and rose again—with the intent of inviting the listener to trust Christ. Evangelism is telling the Good News for the purpose of inviting the sinner to salvation."[1] Consequently, evangelism has two components: (1) sharing information about Jesus Christ and (2) inviting someone to become Christ's disciple. When the Holy Spirit bestows the spiritual gift of evangelism, he gives a believer enhanced love for the spiritually lost and an insatiable passion to plant and water gospel seeds of truth. At the same time, the Spirit grants these believers the ability to reap harvests much more frequently than those who do not have this gift. In other words, believers with the gift of evangelism excel in sharing the gospel and often see positive results when they invite unbelievers to become Christians.

Note that Christians who possess the gift of evangelism have not received that gift in order to serve on behalf of those who do not possess the gift. Evangelism is a responsibility that Christ calls all members of the Body to undertake. In fact, the sharing and reaffirming of gospel truths by those who do not possess the gift of evangelism often prepares unbelievers for an occasion when they encounter an evangelist, who leads that person to actual conversion.

Mark Cahill, an author and evangelist who lives in Stone Mountain, Georgia, is a living example of a child of God who possesses the gift of evangelism. He has shared the gospel with thousands of people in malls, bars, concerts, sporting events, and airplanes. Cahill has a passion for encouraging other Christians to share their faith with others. His preaching and teaching, combined with his books *The One Thing You Can't Do in Heaven* and *One Heartbeat Away,* have inspired hundreds of thousands of Christians to carry out their responsibility to evangelize.[2] His books provide numerous accounts of his evangelistic efforts and confirm his effectiveness in reaping spiritual harvests. They also offer practical ideas for starting evangelistic conversations, sharing your faith, and answering the common questions and objections of unbelievers.

Christians with the gift of evangelism are equipped to preach, teach, speak at revivals and conventions, run street ministries, regularly minister in places sinners typically gather, serve as chaplains, and

---

1. Cecil, *7 Principles of an Evangelistic Life*, 36. See chapter 5 above for more details about evangelism.

2. Visit www.markcahill.org for more information about Mark Cahill and his evangelistic resources.

lead local congregations in neighborhood evangelistic work, along with other tasks of evangelism.

Counseling

The gift of *counseling* allows parishioners to help others toward personal and relational wholeness. A church member graced with the gift of counseling will have some of the capabilities present in persons gifted with prophecy, wisdom, discernment, encouragement, and mercy. Such a person has extraordinary ability to offer emotional comfort, assess and propose solutions to personal problems, discern underlying relational problems, help counselees overcome deeply rooted issues, and maintain strict confidentiality. Like secular counselors, believers graced with the gift of counseling will excel in listening and reconciliation skills and have a genuine drive to assist other people. Unlike secular counselors, they nurture, instruct, and suggest solutions in keeping with Christian values. For instance, a person whom God assigned to counsel a couple with marital problems would not encourage them to seek a divorce if their problems seem insurmountable. Members of the Body who have this gift may minister in official roles, as counselors or pastors for example; however, they may also function without an official title or position in the congregation. In fact, members of the Body will recognize the presence of the gift of counseling and seek the assistance of believers who possess the gift.

In a congregation of my childhood, there was a woman gifted with counseling. She was not part of the pastoral team nor a licensed counselor, but a host of people recognized this gift in her and asked her to help them with their personal and relational needs. Members of the church would call her on the phone, visit her house, or seek private time with her after Sunday morning worship for wise counsel with their relational conflicts. She was so endeared to members of the congregation that we affectionately called her Auntie Caroline.

Saints equipped with the gift of counseling are empowered to serve as informal counselors, premarital counselors, group counselors, youth leaders, visitation team members, cell group leaders, crisis hotline workers, prison ministry teams, altar workers, or as licensed Christian counselors. A host of other ministries would also be appropriate for someone with the gift of counseling.

Leadership

The gift of *leadership* is cited in Romans 12:8. The biblical concept of an every-member ministry, or priesthood of all believers, does not negate the fact that the Lord calls and equips some of his people to serve as leaders. Those assigned to lead are spiritually gifted to envision the direction God has for his people and organize them so that they move toward the goal he intends. They shine as communicators, strategists, and motivators. They are uniquely capable of carrying out complex plans for a local congregation. A God-gifted leader will be "good at delegating responsibilities to maximize effectiveness and can objectively assess which tasks he must do himself and those best done by others team members."[3] A Christian leader may refrain from performing activities they are capable of doing and positioning others to do that work so they can focus on the large picture. The gift of leadership grants believers the ability to stay the course with procedures that work or forsake methods that no longer work. Believers who possess this gift manage to complete tasks and projects, and are inclined to find new endeavors not long after they successfully complete previous undertakings. In terms of leadership style, "Christian leadership is never dogmatic, demagogic, nor dictatorial. Rather, spiritual authority expresses itself in wisdom, tact, example, humility, and service."[4]

People within a congregation tend to naturally follow those graced with the gift of leadership and do not need to be coerced into following them. Gifted leaders have the necessary influence to lead based on their gifting, not due to a title or formal position. In fact, if a person has gained a formal position as leader in a congregation but lacks the spiritual gift to lead, church members will innately lean toward other people in the congregation who do possess the gift of leadership.

---

3. Wollensack, *Called to Be, Called to Do*, 67.

4. Flynn, *19 Gifts of the Spirit*, 141.

Three biblical imperatives are important to consider when examining the gift of leadership: qualifications, humility, and honor. Paul articulates the qualifications for leadership in 1 Timothy 3:2–7:

> Now the overseer is to be above reproach, faithful to his wife, temperate, self-controlled, respectable, hospitable, able to teach, not given to drunkenness, not violent but gentle, not quarrelsome, not a lover of money. He must manage his own family well and see that his children obey him, and he must do so in a manner worthy of full respect. (If anyone does not know how to manage his own family, how can he take care of God's church?) He must not be a recent convert, or he may become conceited and fall under the same judgment as the devil. He must also have a good reputation with outsiders, so that he will not fall into disgrace and into the devil's trap. (NIV)

In light of the public nature of this gift, leaders ought to obey the admonishment Peter gives in 1 Peter 5:5, "All of you, clothe yourselves with humility toward one another, because, 'God opposes the proud but gives grace to the humble.'" In the New Testament, church leaders' work is viewed with such esteem that others are encouraged to honor them:

> And now, friends, we ask you to honor those leaders who work so hard for you, who have been given the responsibility of urging and guiding you along in your obedience. Overwhelm them with appreciation and love! (1 Thess 5:12–13 MSG)

Acts 6 contains an account of effective leadership. When a quarrel developed between Hebraic Jews and Hellenistic Jews over the uneven distribution of food, the twelve apostles successfully met the challenge. Concluding that it was not in the best interest of the church for them to wait tables themselves, the apostles led the men and women of the church to appoint seven qualified men to carry out the responsibility of distributing food fairly to everyone. This allowed the Twelve to focus on prayer and declaring the word of God (vv 1–7).

Christians with the gift of leadership are equipped to serve as pastors, church council members, board of directors, auxiliary leaders, small group leaders, ministers of music, and in a variety of other ministries.

Pastoring

The spiritual gift of *pastoring*, or shepherding, is specifically mentioned in Ephesians 4:11. A man or woman graced with the gift of pastoring is divinely empowered to establish a commitment with a group of Christians to protect them, care for them, oversee their spirituality, and assist them in the development of their God-given ministries. Believers who possess the gift of shepherding will demonstrate varying degrees of the following spiritual gifts: leadership, administration, faith, counseling, prophecy, wisdom, discernment, encouragement, mercy, and evangelism. This enables shepherds to effectively handle an assortment of tasks, such as preaching, teaching, counseling, visiting the sick, and officiating at funerals and weddings. Moreover, members of the Body who hold the gift of pastoring will express a genuine concern for the people in their congregation and community. Clary L. Phelps writes,

> Pastors are to administer the church of Jesus Christ, serve as general overseers of ministries and programs within the church or churches, and nurture the congregation to maturity so they perform the work of ministry.[5]

In fact, part of the biblical calling of a pastor requires that person to equip other Christians so that they can accomplish the tasks that God has for them to fulfill. This job description is detailed in the epistle of Ephesians:

> It was he who gave some to be apostles, some to be prophets, some to be evangelists, and some to be pastors and teachers, to prepare God's people for works of service, so that the body

---

5. Phelps, "Motivation and Empowerment of the Laity," 34.

of Christ may be built up until we all reach unity in the faith and in the knowledge of the Son of God and become mature, attaining to the whole measure of the fullness of Christ. Then we will no longer be infants, tossed back and forth by the waves, and blown here and there by every wind of teaching and by the cunning and craftiness of men in their deceitful scheming. (Eph 4:11–14)

Here Paul encourages apostles, prophets, evangelists, pastors, and teachers to strive for specific results. Each minister within this group knows that they have accomplished their assignment when "the saints are doing the work of ministry, the body of Christ is being built up, the whole body is attaining a unity in the faith, and the community together is expressing the full stature of Christ."[6]

Bloesch points out that "pastors differ from other Christians primarily in their function, but also in the charismatic gifts that enable them to fulfill their special task as ministers of the Word."[7] In fact, the instructions Jesus gave Peter when he reinstated him emphasized the dissemination of Scripture and thus should serve as a guideline for anyone with the gift of pastoring. Jesus commanded Peter to do the following: (1) feed my lambs, (2) tend my sheep, (3) feed the sheep, and (4) follow me (John 21:15–19). In order to do these things, people with the gift of shepherding must minister the Word to those who are spiritual babes, compassionately guard the believers in their care, teach the Word to the spiritually mature, and follow the promptings of Christ. Peter himself would later offer these instructions to pastors himself:

To the elders among you, I appeal as a fellow elder and a witness of Christ's sufferings who also will share in the glory to be revealed: Be shepherds of God's flock that is under your care, watching over them—not because you must, but because you are willing, as God wants you to be; not pursuing dishonest gain, but eager to serve; not lording it over those entrusted

---

6. Ogden, *Unfinished Business*, 132.
7. Bloesch, *Church*, 207.

to you, but being examples to the flock. And when the Chief Shepherd appears, you will receive the crown of glory that will never fade away. (1 Peter 5:1–4 NIV)

Thus far, our discussion of the gift of shepherding has primarily focused on pastoral work as a vocational ministry. However, it is vital to grasp the reality that "though everyone divinely called to the office of pastor will of necessity receive the corresponding gift of pastoring from the Holy Spirit, not everyone who has the gift of pastoring has been called to the office of pastor. You may have the gift of pastoring without being a pastor."[8] People who have the spiritual gift of pastoring but are never called to serve on pastoral staffs are often described by church members as having a "pastor's heart." They love, support, nurture, counsel, encourage, teach, challenge, and motivate the people of God to minister on behalf of the kingdom. While members of the church may never actually refer to them as pastors, these people certainly shepherd the congregation.

Christians gifted by the Spirit for pastoring are endowed to serve as senior, associate, or youth pastors; denominational leaders and auxiliary leaders; Christian convention presidents; presidents of Christian universities; residence hall directors; directors of senior citizen ministries; and in a host of similar ministries.

Deliverance/Exorcism

Parishioners who have received the spiritual gift of *deliverance* are assigned by the Holy Spirit to the task of unleashing others from spiritual bondage. This activity is also referred to as exorcism; for some, however, this word carries a skewed connotation due to Hollywood's portrayal of the fight against demonic forces. Although every child of God has power over evil, believers with the gift of deliverance exercise their Spirit-given ability to cast out demons. A Christian with the gift of deliverance normally has the gift of discernment as well; otherwise, they must rely on believers who have that gift in order to distinguish between situations in which Christian counseling or medical

---

8. Flynn, *19 Gifts of the Spirit*, 77.

intervention is necessary versus those in which a demonic stronghold must be broken prior to counseling or medical intervention.

The reality of demonic enslavement is evident in several biblical accounts, such as Jesus' healing a man in the region of the Gerasenes who had been possessed by an entire legion of demons (Mark 5:1–13). In Acts 8:5–8, we find an account of an early Christ-follower who displays the gift of deliverance:

> Philip went down to the city of Samaria and proclaimed the Messiah to them. The crowds with one accord listened eagerly to what was said by Philip, hearing and seeing the signs that he did, for unclean spirits, crying with loud shrieks, came out of many who were possessed; and many others who were paralyzed or lame were cured. So there was great joy in that city. (NRSV)

Even now, long after the biblical canon has closed, in the unfortunate event that a person becomes spiritually oppressed by the Devil or those aligned with him, Christians armed with the gift of deliverance can be called to restore wholeness.

It is imperative that we not discount or discredit the gift of deliverance, especially in light of the fact that every Christian has a sworn satanic enemy. Paul highlights this truth in his letter to the Ephesians when he writes:

> Put on the whole armor of God, so that you may be able to stand against the wiles of the devil. For our struggle is not against enemies of blood and flesh, but against the rulers, against the authorities, against the cosmic powers of this present darkness, against the spiritual forces of evil in the heavenly places. (Eph 6:11–12 NRSV)

Marshall Tucker is a contemporary example of a believer armed with the gift of deliverance. He pastors New Faith Ministries, a Church of God congregation in Indianapolis, Indiana. For many years, a large portion of his ministry has taken place outside the walls of the church as he has ministered on the street and in prisons. In an interview I conducted with Tucker, he stated, "Deliverance is a gift; not everybody can do it."[9] He went on to provide these additional insights about the gift of deliverance:

1. "You can't counsel [an evil] spirit out; it has to be cast out, and then you counsel the person."
2. People who possess the gift of deliverance have a heightened sense of spiritual discernment.
3. A Christian empowered with this gift should never go in alone to face the Adversary but should always have another believer with them.
4. A Christian with this gift does not have to look for an opportunity to use it. When the time comes, God will guide you in what you ought to do.

Tucker provided details of several encounters he has had with people enslaved by demonic powers. On one occasion, Tucker was standing outside of Wheeler Mission with two other ministers, one of whom also had the gift of deliverance. Suddenly, a man walked up to the minister who did not have the gift of deliverance and forcefully said, "You don't know who I am!" Based on the tone of the man's voice and persona, as well as their own discernment, the two ministers with the gift of deliverance recognized what was happening. They could almost feel the presence of evil in the situation. Prompted by the Holy Spirit, Tucker put his hand on the man's shoulder and said, "I know who you are!" Both ministers with the gift of deliverance began to pray for this man, who fell to the ground as the men continued to pray. When they finished praying, the man's countenance changed. He stood to his feet, apologized, and said, "I don't know what you did, but I want you to come to my house and pray for my wife." Tucker and his colleague did so.

---

9. Marshall Tucker (pastor of New Faith Ministries, Indianapolis, Indiana), phone interview with the author, January 27, 2013.

Christians with the gift of deliverance are equipped for prison ministry, chaplaincy, aiding people with addiction recovery, addressing compulsive behaviors, healing physical illnesses caused by spiritual entanglement, and working in foreign missions, as well as other ministries where the gift of deliverance is likely to be needed.

QUIZ 11
Gifts of the Spirit

Next to each statement, write *T* for true or *F* for false.

_____ 1. In order to lead an unbeliever to Christ, a Christian needs the gift of evangelism.

_____ 2. Evangelism primarily involves appearing to be good and inviting people to church.

_____ 3. A believer graced with the gift of counseling will not encourage an unwed teenager to have an abortion.

_____ 4. Christian counseling should only be provided by an ordained member of clergy.

_____ 5. Christians tend to follow believers graced with the gift of leadership.

_____ 6. People graced with leadership must give special attention to remaining humble.

_____ 7. Commendable pastors spend their time getting others to do ministry.

_____ 8. Once a believer graced with deliverance casts out a demonic spirit, there is no need to provide the victim with psychological counseling.

_____ 9. The gift of deliverance may be particularly useful in foreign mission work.

_____ 10. Since Jesus ascended to the Father, spiritual oppression can no longer occur.

Further Reflection:
Which spiritual gifts mentioned do you believe you have, if any?

As you learned about the details of a particular gift, did a specific member of your church come to mind whom you believe has that gift? Within the next week, share your share your thoughts with them.

CHAPTER 12

Spiritual Gifts Related to Trusting God, Artistic Expression, and Enhancement Endowments

Objectives

1. We will examine a variety of additional spiritual gifts.

2. We will consider whether we have the spiritual gifts discussed.

3. We will assess whether any of these spiritual gifts are exercised by other members of our congregation.

In this session, we continue our exploration of spiritual gifts that fall outside of the manifestations listed in 1 Corinthians 12. Generally speaking, the gifts we survey in this unit relate to trusting God, artistic expression, and endowment enhancement. Spiritual manifestations that relate to trusting God consist of *prayer* and *suffering*. Those that relate to artistic expression are numerous, but here we will explore the gifts of *craftsmanship*, *creativity*, *artistic performance*, and *leading worship*. We will also consider four other gifts of the Spirit that enhance the use of other gifts: *missionary*, *voluntary poverty*, *singleness*, and *pastoral support*.

Prayer

The spiritual gift of *prayer* graces certain believers with a special ability and spiritual anointing to intercede with God in prayer. Every Christian has access to the Father through Jesus Christ and has been graced with the wonderful ability to pray to the God of the universe. All members of the body of Christ can approach the throne of grace being convinced of four foundational truths:

First, *the Lord is sovereign.* Believers can trust the One to whom they make their petitions because God rules the universe, his will cannot be thwarted, and his actions cannot fail. The Psalmist declares, "Our God is in heaven; he does whatever pleases him" (Ps 115:3).

Secondly, *the Lord cares about both the significant and trivial matters of his children.* No prayer request is too big or too small to present to God. In fact, "As a father has compassion on his children, so the LORD has compassion on those who fear him; for he knows how we are formed, he remembers that we are dust" (Ps 103:13–14).

Third, *prayer makes a real difference in our physical world.* According to James, "The prayer of a righteous person is powerful and effective" (James 5:16b). By enabling his people to pray, God invites us to be his co-authors of history.

Fourth, *prayer is a weapon to make war—both defensively and offensively—against the forces of evil in our world.* As 2 Corinthians 10:3–4 puts it, "Though we live in the world, we do not wage war as the world does. The weapons we fight with are not the weapons of the world."

While every believer can confidently approach the Lord based on these principles, certain members of the church graced with the gift of prayer will joyously spend hours praying for their church, community, family, and themselves. They take the prayer concerns of their church newsletter and the issues reported in their local newspaper into their prayer closets. They understand that God may respond to their prayers with "Yes", "No," or "Not now." Even so, "this gift enables Christians to pray for concrete requests over long periods of time, and to receive visible answers far more frequently than other Christians."[1] Furthermore, believers with the gift of prayer often minister behind the scenes

---

1. Schwarz, *3 Colors of Ministry,* 131.

and out of sight, but their gift is as important to the health and victory of the church as all other spiritual gifts.

I know a pastor who has the gift of prayer. He spends several hours a day praying for his family, the congregation he shepherds, the leaders in his region, and for people across the world. He seems able to move the hand of God on the behalf of those he loves and cares for. His enthusiasm and effectiveness in prayer are recognized by many who encounter him. Since he often prays in public as a pastor, members of his church readily associate this gift with him. However, there are thousands of unrecognized heroes and heroines in congregations across the world who uphold their churches in prayer.

Believers who possess the gift of prayer are equipped to lead prayer groups, engage in spiritual warfare, lead prayer vigils, pray for the success of their congregation, visit persons who are unable to attend worship services, in addition to a variety of other ministries.

Suffering

The spiritual gift of *suffering* empowers believers to endure frequent suffering and yet maintain a tenacious faith so that they might encourage other believers to be faithful in the midst of their own struggles. Although every Christian experiences suffering from time to time, Christians with the gift of suffering persist with an unyielding faith, even when others would be greatly tempted to give up. They are able to face discomfort and disappointment without complaining, blaming God, or relinquishing their identity as a child of God. The hardships that people with the gift of suffering experience may be divinely purposed suffering designed to inspire faith in the hearts of others who suffer, but it is not suffering for suffering's sake. The struggles of believers who have the gift of suffering will challenge other believers to stand firm because they can observe what unshakable faith looks like. Christians with the gift of suffering are the kind of people of whom others say, "If they can go through everything they've experienced in life and still have spiritual joy, surely I can endure my smaller version of suffering."

The apostle Paul demonstrated the mindset of someone who has the spiritual gift of suffering when he wrote the following:

What anyone else dares to boast about—I am speaking as a fool—I also dare to boast about. Are they Hebrews? So am I. Are they Israelites? So am I. Are they Abraham's descendants? So am I. Are they servants of Christ? (I am out of my mind to talk like this.) I am more. I have worked much harder, been in prison more frequently, been flogged more severely, and been exposed to death again and again. Five times I received from the Jews the forty lashes minus one. Three times I was beaten with rods, once I was stoned, three times I was ship-wrecked, I spent a night and a day in the open sea, I have been constantly on the move. I have been in danger from rivers, in danger from bandits, in danger from my own countrymen, in danger from Gentiles; in danger in the city, in danger in the country, in danger at sea; and in danger from false brothers. I have labored and toiled and have often gone without sleep; I have known hunger and thirst and have often gone without food; I have been cold and naked. Besides everything else, I face daily the pressure of my concern for all the churches. Who is weak, and I do not feel weak? Who is led into sin, and I do not inwardly burn?

If I must boast, I will boast of the things that show my weakness. The God and Father of the Lord Jesus, who is to be praised forever, knows that I am not lying. In Damascus the governor under King Aretas had the city of the Damascenes guarded in order to arrest me. But I was lowered in a basket from a window in the wall and slipped through his hands. (2 Cor 11:21b–33)

The perseverance of believers with this spiritual gift allows them to inspire visitors as the encouraging recipient of home, hospital, or nursing home visits; as ministers in foreign missions; as leaders of prayer groups and church plants; and in other diverse ministries.

Craftsmanship

Craftsmanship is the "extraordinary ability to use physical materials and artistic skills to create, mold, carve, sculpt, draw, design, paint, repair, or photograph items necessary for spiritual nurture, faith development, and caring ministries."[2] Christians who possess the gift of craftsmanship have the special ability to create or alter objects that convey religious meaning. They may also fashion physical articles used for Christian purposes, such as pulpits, sanctuary chairs, and baptismal pools. Hence, the difference between a secular craftsman and a Christian with the gift of craftsmanship lies in the purpose and effect of the objects they produce. A believer with this gift will create physical objects on multiple occasions that inspire, inform, challenge, or change other believers for the better. They may also use their gifting evangelistically.

A good Old Testament picture of craftsmanship can be found in Exodus 31:1–11, which says that Bezalel, Aholiab, and Ahisamach were filled "with the Spirit of God, with wisdom, with understanding, with knowledge and with all kinds of skills—to make artistic designs for work in gold, silver and bronze, to cut and set stones, to work in wood, and to engage in all kinds of crafts" (NIV). God gave them these special abilities so they could make the tent of meeting, the ark of the covenant, and all other tent furnishings for the Israelites' portable worship center. Christians possessing the gift of craftsmanship can be found outside the Bible as well. One example is the artist known to the world as Rembrandt. His painting *The Return of the Prodigal Son* so moved a Catholic priest named Henri J.M. Nouwen that he spent several days in front of the painting meditating on it. Nouwen would go on to write a book titled *Return of the Prodigal Son: A Story of Homecoming.*

Members of the church graced with the gift of craftsmanship have the special ability to build worship furniture, design or renovate church buildings, create paintings to inspire homebound believers, and do a host of other things that require creative imagination and great dexterity.

---

2. Bryant, *Rediscovering Our Spiritual Gifts*, 67.

Creativity

Closely related to it is the gift of *creativity*, which allows Christians to engage in artistic expression for kingdom purposes. A Christian graced with this gift uses their imagination to produce a wide range of artistic renderings. Such a person may write Christian books, music, and poems; design worship choreography for praise dancers, mime teams, and sign-language choirs; and design websites, social media pages, and church marketing materials. As with the gift of craftsmanship, the purpose and effectiveness of the gift of creativity distinguish it from secular forms of artistry. For instance, a secular choreographer will create a dance in order to entertain, while a person with the spiritual gift of creativity will choreograph scenes that uplift, challenge, and point persons toward Jesus Christ. The gift of creativity is confirmed when members of the church describe such persons' work as powerful, anointed, or a blessing.

My wife, Precious Ann Earley, has been graced with the gift of creativity, which she has used to benefit the Metropolitan Church of God in a variety of ways. She has designed multifaceted Christmas programs featuring black-light mime, praise dancing, singing, and drama. She has designed our church directory, website, Facebook page, letterhead, and brochures. She has even developed artistic lessons for our children's church program.

Believers with this gift may exercise it in an infinite variety of ways—create church publications, write press releases, compose church radio-commercial scripts, write Christian comedy routines, compose music for orchestras and choirs, and so on.

Artistic Performance

The next spiritual gift to be explored is *artistic performance*. Individuals with this gift perform the creations of those who possess the gift of creativity. The gift of artistic performance empowers a person to sing, act, play instruments, dance, and mime to the glory of the Lord. Put another way, someone with the gift of creativity might choreograph a praise dance, while another person with the gift of artistic performance might present that dance during a worship service. While some artistic performers also have the gift of creativity, they may solely focus on performing what another believer has constructed. Using a basketball analogy, some coaches are able both to coach and play, while others only give their attention to coaching. Likewise, some creators perform their creations, while others focus on creation so other Christians can use their gifting to perform. The gift of performance also equips church choir, band, and orchestra directors to lead others as they sing or play worship music.

The book of 1 Chronicles mentions several specific ministries that require the gift of artistic performance, including vocalists (15:19), instrumentalists (15:20), and choir directors (15:22). Believers who have the gift of artistic performance are equipped to engage in various forms of worship arts, such as singing with the choir or praise team, singing solos, playing instrumental solos, or joining the church band or orchestra.

Leading Worship

Another special ability given by the Holy Spirit for the edification of the church is that of *leading worship*. Worship leaders can guide and inspire other Christians during corporate worship so that they have an authentic encounter with God. Without manipulating the congregation, gifted worship leaders can move others from watching to worshiping. At times, they will verbally prompt worshipers by calling attention to the attributes of God and the things he has done. At other times, they may share their private worship publicly. As a worship leader offers praise and worship to God during a service, they spur other Christians to exalt the Lord with them. Whereas a pianist may use his gift of performance to play the piano for the glory of God, someone gifted in leading worship will coordinate the gathered people of God to create a communal expression of praise that is pleasing unto him. Children of God who have the gift of leading worship have a passion for uplifting public and private worship. In fact, the sense of satisfaction they experience while successfully encouraging others to worship is second only to what they experience when worshiping God in private.

Choir directors with the spiritual gift of performance may also have the gift of leading worship. In this instance, they might use both gifts to direct the choir and band members, or play an instrument, while they encourage the community of believers to praise the Lord. This is not always the case, however. A choir director who does not have the gift of leading worship will focus on the choir and band's performance without verbally engaging the congregation or attempting to exhort them toward more passionate worship. Like all other spiritual gifts, the Holy Spirit will only grace a member of a particular congregation with the gift of leading worship and create an opportunity for them to minister in this capacity if he deems it necessary.

Moreover, a worship leader will plan the worship service, either alone or with a team of worship leaders and performers. As part of this planning, a person gifted to lead worship will consider hymns and gospel songs in a variety of styles and plan to use those that are most likely to assist the church in its expression of gratitude and adoration for the Lord. The gifted worship leader selects music that not only addresses other worshipers but also addresses God.

Joyce Terry is an example of a person graced with the gift of leading worship. She serves as the worship leader at the First Church of God in Columbus, Ohio, as well as worship leader for a variety of church conventions and meetings. Gifted both as a worship leader and performer, Terry is an excellent singer who uses her voice as a catalyst to encourage other believers to participate in corporate worship. Her gifting allows her to help others perceive the presence and power of God, and to respond to him in a manner worthy of his name.

Members of the Body entrusted with the gift of leading worship may lead worship in local congregations or local, national, and international church events; they may also exercise this gift in more intimate settings, such as small-group Bible studies, nursing homes, or hospital and college chapels.

Missionary

The first enhancement gift to be explored is the gift of *missionary*. This gift enables believers to minister effectively in a culture or social context that is quite different from their own. Christians with this gift have the ability to learn a new culture, assimilate themselves into it, and successfully gain the trust and acceptance of the people they intend to serve. In order to do this, they will invoke their innate ability to learn and communicate with foreigners in their own language. Moreover, they are eager to cross cultural boundaries and minister to people unlike them.

The gift of missionary is most often used by persons who serve in other countries; however, this gift can open doors of opportunity to minister to people of our own country as well. For example, a believer born and raised in a rural area of the South will likely need the gift of missionary to minister to inner-city youth in the North.

A Christian who possess the gift of missionary may also need a wide range of other spiritual gifts to minister effectively to people of different cultures and contexts. Such cross-cultural ministry gifts might be prophecy, evangelism, encouragement, mercy, service, craftsmanship, creativity, deliverance, or pastoring. However, this is worth noting:

> If no missionary gift exists, the person will have to employ his gifts in his own familiar culture. The believer with the gift of evangelism, but minus the missionary ability, will have to evangelize in his own culture. To witness competently across cultural lines mandates the missionary gift. Wherever a cultural gap exists, the missionary gift is needed if that person is to survive the strange environment, remain on the field, and do an effective piece of work.[3]

Believers who have been graced with this gift can be quite successful as international pastors, evangelists, physicians, lawyers, community builders, church planters, and staff members of ministries designed to serve marginalized people.

---

3. Flynn, *19 Gifts of the Spirit*, 52–53.

Voluntary Poverty

The second enhancement gift we shall examine is the gift of *voluntary poverty*. Voluntary poverty enables believers to joyfully live a simple life, well beneath their financial means, so they can contribute more substantially toward kingdom efforts. Paul alludes to this practice as he describes true Christian love in 1 Corinthians 13:3, "If I give away all my possessions, and if I hand over my body so that I may boast, but do not have love, I gain nothing" (NRSV). When the Holy Spirit confers the gift of voluntary poverty on certain believers, they "do not consider themselves poor or dislike material possessions; they prefer to be free of these things so that they can spend more of their time, energies, influence, and spiritual resources to minister."[4] While Christians with the gift of voluntary poverty may have the gift of giving as well, believers with the gift of giving often do not chose to live a life of poverty for ministry purposes.

It is also important to note that the spiritual gift is one of *voluntary* poverty. Experiencing poverty is not in itself proof that someone has this spiritual gift; however, we see this gift demonstrated in the lives of people who could live more lavish lifestyles but instead prefer to give their time, energy, and money for the glory of God. Further note that the gift of detachment from worldly possessions, along with the stress associated with obtaining and maintaining them, is usually paired with other forms of ministry gifts. In other words, the church is not strengthened by members who are poor for the sake of being poor.

Mother Theresa is an example of a person blessed to serve the world through voluntary poverty. She chose to live in poverty so that her time and resources could be used to minister to the world's poorest people. Parishioners graced with this gift are equipped to serve in foreign missions, minister to marginalized people, serve the homeless, and engage in a host of other ministries.

Singleness

The third enhancement gift is the gift of *singleness*. This gift is defined as "the extraordinary ability to offer God and the church a

---

4. Penn, *Rediscovering Our Spiritual Gifts*, 68.

life unbound by marriage and free of sexual frustrations and social attachments so that one may spend the time and energy necessary for building up the church."[5] The Greek word for singleness is *αγαμος,* which means unmarried, unbound, or unattached.[6]

Similar to other enhancement gifts, the gift of singleness becomes fruitful when it is coupled with other gifts. Singleness in and of itself is not a spiritual gift. In other words, not every unmarried person has the gift of singleness. A person who is contentedly single, however, because they enjoy having more time to serve the body of Christ with other spiritual gifts, likely possesses the gift of singleness. Although individual Christians may delay marriage in order to accomplish certain ministry goals, the Spirit does not temporarily grace members of the Body with the gift of singleness. Instead, believers graced with this gift willingly choose never to be married. Christians who are discontent being single or cringe at the notion of remaining forever unmarried are demonstrating the fact that they do not have the spiritual gift of singleness.

Commenting on the church's need to accept the spiritual gift of singleness, Charles Bryant writes: "No small amount of guilt has been imposed on many persons who wish to remain single. Our perception of persons who remain single usually carries a stigma resulting from bad theology and church practices that assert the ultimate purpose for life it to reproduce a like kind."[7] As a result, some Christians who would have been happier and more productive for the kingdom as unmarried individuals have grudgingly entered marriage.

Paul alludes to having the gift of singleness himself. After he instructs married couples to fulfill their sexual responsibilities toward one another, he writes, "I wish that all of you were as I am. But each of you has your own gift from God; one has this gift, another has that" (1 Cor 7:7 NIV). He goes on to express the benefits of singleness,

---

5. Bryant, *Rediscovering Our Spiritual Gifts,* 135. See 1 Corinthians 7:32–38.

6. Ibid.

7. Ibid.

I would like you to be free from concern. An unmarried man is concerned about the Lord's affairs—how he can please the Lord. But a married man is concerned about the affairs of this world—how he can please his wife—and his interests are divided. An unmarried woman or virgin is concerned about the Lord's affairs: Her aim is to be devoted to the Lord in both body and spirit. But a married woman is concerned about the affairs of this world—how she can please her husband. I am saying this for your own good, not to restrict you, but that you may live in a right way in undivided devotion to the Lord.

If anyone is worried that he might not be acting honorably toward the virgin he is engaged to, and if his passions are too strong and he feels he ought to marry, he should do as he wants. He is not sinning. They should get married. But the man who has settled the matter in his own mind, who is under no compulsion but has control over his own will, and who has made up his mind not to marry the virgin—this man also does the right thing. So then, he who marries the virgin does right, but he who does not marry her does better. (1 Cor 7:32–38 NIV)

When the church accepts the spiritual gift of singleness as being truly God-given, believers who are so graced will be freer to identify this gift within themselves and strengthen the effectiveness of the other spiritual gifts they possess, due to the freedom of singleness.

Pastoral Support

The fourth enhancement gift we want to explore is the gift of *pastoral support*. This is essentially an enhancement of the gift of helps. Through the spiritual gift of pastoral support, parishioners encourage and enable their pastor to carry out his or her ministry assignment. Any believer graced with the gift of helps can assist the pastor, of course, but someone who has the gift of pastoral support can develop closer relationships with the pastor and thereby help in more personal ways. In the sense that senior pastors are the servants of all, we might say that a person graced with the gift of pastoral support serves the servant in chief. Christians with this gift joyously aid their pastors by praying for them daily, assisting them in times of congregational crisis, defending the pastors against slander when appropriate and necessary, helping the pastors meet emergency financial obligations, and ministering to the pastors' emotional and spiritual needs when they experience wounds in their personal lives, such as the loss of their loved ones. Persons graced with this gift will also tend to aid the pastor when he or she is physically ill. The gift of pastoral support is especially beneficial to older pastors and those who serve large congregations.

Believers with the gift of pastoral support feel that they participate personally in the success of their pastor's ministry. They serve as sounding boards, keeping the pastor informed about the thoughts and opinions of the congregation so that wise decisions can be made. To put it bluntly, pastoral supporters let their pastors know what they hear through the grapevine. Trusted by their pastor and skilled in maintaining confidence, pastoral supporters privately affirm their pastor's appropriate actions and offer constructive feedback when improvement is needed.

Similar to the gift of evangelism, this gift does not negate the responsibility of other Christians to support their pastor. Believers who have the gift of pastoral support, however, are inspired and enabled to assist their pastors in ways that makes pastoral work a joy. It appears that Mark used the gift of pastoral support to help Paul in his ministry. In 2 Timothy 4:11, Paul writes, "Get Mark and bring him with you, because he is helpful to me in my ministry."

A modern-day example of the gift of pastoral support is Joseph Marshall, who has served the senior pastors at both Covenant Faith Church of God in Chicago, Illinois, and First Church of God in Inglewood, California. He sees his ministry to the pastor as a ministry to the congregation as a whole. Marshall's love, loyalty, and ministry to his pastors has indeed been beneficial to them, their families, and the congregations they serve. Church members who possess the gift of pastoral support are equipped to serve the pastor in a variety of formal and informal ways to strengthen their ministry to the congregation.

QUIZ 12
Gifts of the Spirit

Next to each statement, write *T* for true or *F* for false.

_____ 1. Believers who possess the gift of prayer tend to enjoy spending hours in prayer.

_____ 2. Christians who do not have the gift of prayer will not have their prayers answered.

_____ 3. The experience of hardship means a believer has the gift of suffering.

_____ 4. A believer graced with the gift of suffering faces tribulations with unyielding faith.

_____ 5. The gift of deliverance is used to make believers pass out in order to remind the congregation of the Spirit's power.

_____ 6. The gift of discernment should be used alongside the gift of deliverance.

_____ 7. The entire body of Christ benefits from the gift of pastoral support.

_____ 8. Until married, every believer possesses the gift of singleness.

_____ 9. Believers with meager means are not likely to have the gift of voluntary poverty.

_____ 10. A person with the gift of craftsmanship is equipped to lead a choir.

Further Reflection:

Which spiritual gifts mentioned do you believe you have, if any?

As you listened to the details of a particular gift, did a specific member of your church come to mind whom you believe has that gift? Within the next week, share your thoughts with them.

Conclusion

Not long ago I was at a Christian youth convention waiting for an elevator. The hotel that hosted the convention was also hosting attendees of a major college football bowl, so the area around the elevator was quite packed. Each time an elevator opened, swarms of people tried to jam themselves into it in an attempt to reach higher floors. Eventually I remembered that as a staff member of the church convention, I was given access to a different elevator that would allow me to reach my destination quicker than I could using the normal mode of transportation. I took advantage of this privilege. As it turns out, the service elevator was the one that accelerated my journey.

In a world where people are willing to push and shove their way to the top, Christians have privileged access to a different mode of travel. Since every believer has received at least one spiritual gift, we can step into God's service elevator, which will accelerate us toward our God-ordained assignment. As we exercise our spiritual gifts and refuse to stand idly by as other believers serve, we please God, meet the needs of others, and experience the joy of godly obedience.

I pray that this examination of every-member ministry and spiritual gifting motivates you to assume your rightful role as one of your congregation's servants. You are uniquely equipped to minister to other people for God's glory through the spiritual gift(s) the Holy Spirit has graciously placed within you. While several other believers may possess the same gift(s) you possess, only you can carry out your God-assigned tasks through your unique personality. Will you be counted among the multitude of Christians who lovingly render their spiritual gifts and natural talents to one another and thereby answer God's call to serve?

Appendix A
1 Corinthians 12

SPIRITUAL GIFTS

[1] Now about spiritual gifts, brothers, I do not want you to be ignorant. [2] You know that when you were pagans, somehow or other you were influenced and led astray to mute idols. [3] Therefore I tell you that no one who is speaking by the Spirit of God says, "Jesus be cursed," and no one can say, "Jesus is Lord," except by the Holy Spirit.

[4] There are different kinds of gifts, but the same Spirit. [5] There are different kinds of service, but the same Lord. [6] There are different kinds of working, but the same God works all of them in all men.

[7] Now to each one the manifestation of the Spirit is given for the common good. [8] To one there is given through the Spirit the message of wisdom, to another the message of knowledge by means of the same Spirit, [9] to another faith by the same Spirit, to another gifts of healing by that one Spirit, [10] to another miraculous powers, to another prophecy, to another distinguishing between spirits, to another speaking in different kinds of tongues, and to still another the interpretation of tongues. [11] All these are the work of one and the same Spirit, and he gives them to each one, just as he determines.

ONE BODY, MANY PARTS

[12] The body is a unit, though it is made up of many parts; and though all its parts are many, they form one body. So it is with Christ. [13] For we were all baptized by one Spirit into one body--whether Jews or Greeks, slave or free—and we were all given the one Spirit to drink.

[14] Now the body is not made up of one part but of many. [15] If the foot should say, "Because I am not a hand, I do not belong to the body," it would not for that reason cease to be part of the body. [16] And

if the ear should say, "Because I am not an eye, I do not belong to the body," it would not for that reason cease to be part of the body. [17] If the whole body were an eye, where would the sense of hearing be? If the whole body were an ear, where would the sense of smell be? [18] But in fact God has arranged the parts in the body, every one of them, just as he wanted them to be. [19] If they were all one part, where would the body be? [20] As it is, there are many parts, but one body.

[21] The eye cannot say to the hand, "I don't need you!" And the head cannot say to the feet, "I don't need you!" [22] On the contrary, those parts of the body that seem to be weaker are indispensable, [23] and the parts that we think are less honorable we treat with special honor. And the parts that are unpresentable are treated with special modesty, [24] while our presentable parts need no special treatment. But God has combined the members of the body and has given greater honor to the parts that lacked it, [25] so that there should be no division in the body, but that its parts should have equal concern for each other. [26] If one part suffers, every part suffers with it; if one part is honored, every part rejoices with it.

[27] Now you are the body of Christ, and each one of you is a part of it. [28] And in the church God has appointed first of all apostles, second prophets, third teachers, then workers of miracles, also those having gifts of healing, those able to help others, those with gifts of administration, and those speaking in different kinds of tongues. [29] Are all apostles? Are all prophets? Are all teachers? Do all work miracles? [30] Do all have gifts of healing? Do all speak in tongues ? Do all interpret? [31] But eagerly desire the greater gifts. And now I will show you the most excellent way.

Appendix B

QUIZ ANSWERS

Chapter 1

1. False. All believers perform real ministry in the kingdom by using their spiritual gifts.

2. False. Pastors, priests, and ministers cannot replace members of the body, whom God calls to serve personally in ministry.

3. True. Faithful Christians have real relationships with God, love for one another, and are committed to serving others.

4. False. A church that encourages the active participation of all its members will likely be effective.

5. True. All believers have access to God through prayer and have been made ambassadors of Christ.

6. True. Every believer is given at least one spiritual gift upon salvation and thus becomes a minister/servant.

7. False. There is no substitute for personally serving others in Christ's name.

8. False. Declining congregations tend to have clergy-centered ministries.

9. True. One aspect of a Christian's inheritance is involvement in ministry.

10. True. Your ministry contribution is as essential as all others, because God's design for ministry requires every member of the church to be involved in its ministry.

Chapter 2

1. False. All believers have at least one spiritual gift.

2. True. Every believer can be great because each one can offer their spiritual gift(s) to others.

3. True. The Holy Spirit expresses his care and concern for the church by gracing its members with spiritual gifts.

4. False. Women belong in ministry because of their spiritual gifts.

5. False. Christians should be proactive in using their spiritual gift(s).

6. False. In addition to having one's spiritual and physical needs met, Christians are to use their spiritual gifts and natural talents as they pursue God's will.

7. True. The Spirit intends for each believer to participate in every-member ministry by offering their spiritual gifts.

8. True. Spiritual gifts are not signs of merit.

9. False. Christians should not feel embarrassed or exalted when they compare the number of spiritual gifts they have with the gifts of other believers.

10. True. The Holy Spirit spreads the spiritual gifts a congregation needs across all of its members.

Chapter 3

1. True. Spiritual gifts are special abilities whose purpose is to edify the church.

2. False. Christians are expected to make unique contributions through a diversity of spiritual gifts.

3. True. A believer possesses a spiritual gift solely because the Holy Spirit has graced them with it.

4. False. Spiritual gifts are given by God and not earned.

5. False. Spiritual gifts are not evidence of a believer's spiritual maturity.

6. True. Spiritual maturity and training can directly influence the effectiveness of a spiritual gift.

7. False. Believers can possess spiritual gifts before they know what they are or how to use them.

8. True. The Spirit supplies spiritual gifts so the church can be edified.

9. False. Spiritual gifts edify the church, while natural talents bless all humanity.

10. True. There is no spiritual gift that every believer possesses; however, every believer is required to have the fruit of the Spirit and fulfill their Christian duties.

Chapter 4

1. True. An important part of every believer's spiritual journey is to render service to others by exercising their spiritual gift(s).

2. False. Prayer is essential throughout the gift discovery process.

3. True. If a Christian is not fully receptive to God's will for their life they are more likely to over focus on a gift they do not have or overlook a gift they do.

4. False. Believers should never withhold their spiritual gifts from other members of the body.

5. True. The more a Christian knows about the variety of spiritual gifts, the easier it will be for them to identify the spiritual gifts they have.

6. False. Conversations with other believers will assist in discovering one's spiritual gifts.

7. False. The results of a spiritual gift assessment should be considered alongside the information gathered in the other six steps of the gift discovery process.

8. False. Spiritual gifts can be used on a trial basis in ways that avoid embarrassing the experimenter.

9. True. The presence of a spiritual gift allows a believer to be successful in a certain aspect of ministry over time.

10. True. When a Christian has been graced with a spiritual gift, the members of the body will formally or informally validate the presence of that gift and accept its rendering.

Chapter 5

1. True. Christ is the supreme ruler of the church.

2. False. Your pastor does not own your congregation. Jesus Christ's church has the ability to be the greatest change agent in the world.

3. True. A congregation separated from Christ is disconnected from the source of life.

4. False. The Holy Spirit assigns Christians to specific ministries through the spiritual gifts he equips them with.

5. True. Once people's earthly needs are met, they will likely be more open to having their spiritual needs met.

6. True. Authentic Christian ministry addresses personal sin and societal sin through evangelism and social action.

7. False. Believers must live as Christ followers inside and outside of the voting booth.

8. True. The Lord requires righteousness in the hearts and in the social structures of men and women.

9. False. When people accept the Lord as their Savior, it will not automatically reverse the outcomes of sinful structures that men and women have set up.

10. False. The church should be in the forefront in dealing with problems of human dignity, social empowerment, and economic justice.

Chapter 6

1. True. According to Jesus, the two greatest commandments involve loving God and loving one's neighbor.

2. True. Discord among believers makes the rendering and receiving of spiritual gifts very difficult.

3. False. Spiritual gifts rendered publically and privately have equal importance.

4. True. Local congregations only achieve their greatest potential when every member of the church is involved in ministry.

5. False. Christians are all interdependent within God's design for ministry.

6. False. Unhealthy relationships among Christians can hinder the successful use of spiritual gifts.

7. False. When a member of the church experiences difficult times, they should draw closer to other believers so they can benefit from the love, support, and spiritual gifts of fellow believers.

8. False. No spiritual gift can be earned.

9. True. A believer cannot render their spiritual gifts to him or herself.

10. True. When a member fails to render their gift, the whole church misses out on a gift the Holy Spirit intended for it.

Chapter 7

1. False. Pastors who endeavor to do the work of ministry by themselves are subject to burnout and ineffectiveness.

2. False. Every believer who appropriately uses their spiritual gift(s) is qualified to render effective ministry.

3. False. Members of the body cannot minister vicariously through their pastor.

4. True. When a pastor equips a person for ministry, they help them offer the spiritual gift(s) the Holy Spirit has placed in the them.

5. True. The Holy Spirit puts pastors in place to equip others for ministry.

6. False. Christians who want to use their spiritual gifts must derive their power and authority from the Holy Spirit.

7. False. A healthy church is one in which the majority of members function in their God-assigned ministry.

8. True. Laypersons are empowered by the Holy Spirit to be successful in ministry.

9. True. Pastors are called to equip believers for ministry, but ultimately the source of ministry empowerment is the Holy Spirit.

10. True. Healthy pastors trust the Holy Spirit to properly empower all believers to successfully participate in ministry.

Chapter 8

1. True. Disciples of Christ should serve for the glory of God inside and outside their local congregation.

2. False. There are a variety of ways spiritual gifting can be used outside the church for kingdom purposes.

3. True. Marginalized people are behind in the race of life and need help catching up with their counterparts.

4. False. Congregations should offer sacred and secular programing to their communities as they work to promote God's will on earth as it is in heaven.

5. False. At times a Christian's resources are best used in individual development, community development, or structural transformation efforts.

6. True. Christ's followers ought to help people secure eternal life and equitable earthly life.

7. True. Jesus said, "Whatever you did for one of the *least* of these brothers and sisters of mine, you did for me" (Matt 25:40 NIV).

8. False. Jesus was not afforded the opportunity to vote during his earthy ministry; however, his present-day followers can cast their votes in ways that honor his values.

9. True. Christians must see all humans as the neighbors we are commanded to love.

10. False. A local congregation should use the opportunities afforded it to make a positive difference in the world.

Chapter 9

1. True. No biblical passage claims to provide a definitive list of spiritual gifts.

2. True. A person who possesses the gift of wisdom is equipped to detect and fix problems in the congregation.

3. False. The Holy Spirit gives the gift of knowledge to the educated or uneducated as he pleases.

4. False. A believer only needs saving faith, not the spiritual gift of faith, to receive salvation.

5. False. If a congregation does not have an individual(s) with the spiritual gift of healing, they should not have a healing ministry.

6. True. The terms *preacher* and *prophet* can be used interchangeably.

7. True. The gift of tongues allows communication through a language unknown to the speaker, hearer, or both.

8. True. The biblical guidelines for the appropriate use of the gift of tongues in a church setting requires interpretation of the message spoken in tongues.

9. False. An individual's natural talents do not automatically mirror their spiritual gifting.

10. False. Christians who possess the gift of discernment are best equipped to distinguish between legitimate and illegitimate preaching.

Chapter 10

1. False. All Christians are all required to fulfill the Christian duty of tithing, whether or not they have the spiritual gift of giving.

2. False. Believers who possess the gift of giving give without expecting anything in return from God or other believers.

3. True. Strangers and newcomers benefit from the love and attention they receive from Christians graced with the gift of hospitality.

4. False. People with the gift of hospitality are equipped to minister in a wide range of church activities and need not be limited to the usher's or greeter's ministry.

5. False. The Holy Spirit does not distribute the gift of mercy so that believers can be abused.

6. True. God is compassionate and willing to help those who struggle with habits and hang-ups.

7. True. Believers graced with the gift of hospitality tend to enjoy hosting large numbers of guests in their home.

8. False. Believers who have the gift of service do not take on church assignments hoping to gain fame or fortune.

9. True. The gift of encouragement allows members of the body to positively motivate others to remain obedient and faithful.

10. True. The gift of service can be used appropriately in many different ways.

Chapter 11

1. False. The gift of evangelism is not required for ordinary Christians to share their faith and lead non-believers to Christ.

2. False. Evangelism primarily involves sharing information and an invitation to Christian discipleship.

3. True. A members of the church who posses the gift of counseling will offer counsel that aligns with biblical values.

4. False. Christian counseling should only be provided by persons who have been graced with the gift of counseling.

5. True. Christians innately follow the members of the church who have been gifted to lead.

6. True. Christian leaders who are humble vaccinate themselves against the pitfalls and woes of arrogance.

7. True. Pastors who equip others for ministry ought to be applauded.

8. False. The gift of deliverance enables believers to cast out evil spirits, which lays the necessary groundwork for Christian counseling.

9. True. Foreign missionaries who encounter demonic forces are aided by those who possess the gift of deliverance.

10. False. Until Christ returns, humans are still susceptible to demonic influences.

Chapter 12

1. True. Believers who have the gift of prayer love spending abundant time in prayer.

2. False. All Christians have access to God and can expect their prayers to be answered even if they do not have the spiritual gift of prayer.

3. False. The experience of hardship in and of itself does not point towards the presence of the gift of suffering.

4. True. Christians who possess the gift of suffering maintain a dogged faith in the best and worse of times.

5. False. The gift of deliverance is used to free persons from demonic oppression.

6. True. The gift of discernment should be used to understand if a person is suffering from physical, emotional, or demonic duress.

7. True. The entire church benefits from pastoral support because a pastor who has her or his needs attended to is in a better position to serve others.

8. False. The gift of singleness is a permanent gift that allows believers to remain contentedly unmarried.

9. True. The gift of voluntary poverty allows believers with abundant resources to forfeit their wealth for kingdom purposes.

10. False. The spiritual gift of artistic performance enables a Christian to lead a choir.

Spiritual Gift Index

Bibliography

Aukerman, John, Joseph Smythe, and Debbie Starr. *Christian Relationships: God's Design for You and Me.* Pittsburgh, PA: The LOGOS Ministry, 2005.

Bloesch, Donald. *The Church: Sacraments, Worship, Ministry, Mission.* Downers Grove, IL: Intervarsity Press, 2002.

Blomberg, Craig. *1 Corinthians.* The NIV Application Commentary. Grand Rapids, MI: Zondervan, 1994.

Brueggemann, Walter. "Exodus." In *The New Interpreter's Bible*, vol. 1. Nashville, TN: Abingdon Press, 1994.

Bradford, John "The Phrase Finder." http://www.phrases.org.uk/meanings/there-but-for-the-grace-of-god.html (accessed January 23, 2013).

Bryant, Charles V. *Rediscovering Our Spiritual Gifts: Building Up the Body of Christ Through the Gifts of the Spirit.* Nashville, TN: Upper Room Books, 1991.

Callen, Barry L., ed. and comp. *Following Our Lord: Understanding the Beliefs and Practices of the Church of God Movement (Anderson).* Anderson, IN: Warner Press, 2008.

Cecil, Douglas M. *The 7 Principles of an Evangelistic Life.* Chicago, IL: Moody Publishers, 2003.

Dulin, Robert O., Jr. "Walking Through the Book of Colossians: The Preeminent Christ." Midweek Bible Study Handout for the Metropolitan Church of God, September 25, 2007.

Enns, Peter. *Exodus.* The NIV Application Commentary. Grand Rapids, MI: Zondervan, 2000.

Fannie Lou Hamer Political Action Committee. "About Us." http://www.flhpac.org/index.php?id=1 (accessed December 5, 2012).

Fee, Gordon D. *The First Epistle to the Corinthians.* The New International Commentary on the New Testament. Grand Rapids, MI: William B. Eerdmans, 1987.

Flynn, Leslie B. *19 Gifts of the Spirit: Which Do You Have? Are You Using Them?* Colorado Springs, CO: David C. Cook, 2004.

Fortune, Don and Katie. *Discover Your God-Given Gifts.* Grand Rapids, MI: Chosen Books, 1987.

Garland, David E. *1 Corinthians.* Baker Exegetical Commentary on the New Testament. Grand Rapids, MI: Baker Academic, 2003.

Huber, Randal Robert. "Advancing the Placement of Women in the Church of God." DMin diss., Anderson University School of Theology, 2003.

King, Martin Luther, Jr. "The Drum Major Instinct-Martin Luther King," BlackWebPortal. http://www.blackwebportal.com/wire/DA.cfm ?ArticleID=513 (accessed August 27, 2007).

Luther, Martin. *Works of Martin Luther.* Philadelphia, PA: Westminster, 1943.

McRae, William. *Dynamics of Spiritual Gifts.* Grand Rapids, MI: Zondervan, 1976.

Nouwen, Henri J.M. *Return of the Prodigal Son: A Story of Homecoming.* New York, NY: Doubleday, 1992.

Ogden, Greg. *Unfinished Business: Returning the Ministry to the People of God.* Grand Rapids, MI: Zondervan, 2003.

Penn, John I. *Rediscovering Our Spiritual Gifts: A Workbook.* Nashville, TN: Upper Room Books, 1996.

Phelps, Clary L. "Motivation and Empowerment of the Laity in a Small Congregation." DMin diss., United Theological Seminary, 1997.

Richardson, W. Franklin. *The Power in the Pew.* Nashville, TN: Townsend Press, 1986.

Ruffcorn, Kevin. "Recovering the Priesthood of All Believers: A Study of the Discovery and Deployment of Spiritual Gifts for Service and Their Effect on the Individual's Assurance of God's Grace and Awareness of Neighbor's Need." DMin diss., Asbury Theological Seminary, 2004.

Schwarz, Christian. *The 3 Colors of Ministry: A Trinitarian Approach to Identifying and Developing Your Spiritual Gifts.* St Charles, IL: ChurchSmart Resources, 2001.

Shumate, Charles R., and Sherrill D. Hayes, eds. *Discover Your Gifts: Leader's Notebook.* Anderson, IN: Warner Press, 1990.

Sider, Ronald. *Good News and Good Works: A Theology for the Whole Gospel.* Grand Rapids, MI: Baker Books, 1993.

Sider, Ronald, and Diane Knippers. *Toward an Evangelical Public Policy.* Grand Rapids, MI: Baker Books, 2005.

Sider, Ronald, Philip N. Olson, and Heidi Unruh. *Churches That Make a Difference: Reaching Your Community with Good News and Good Works.* Grand Rapids, MI: Baker Books, 2002.

Starnes, Darryl B., Sr. "Equipping the Saints for the Work of Ministry: Teaching Adults to Share Their Faith at Evans Metropolitan African Methodist Episcopal Zion Church, Bennettsville, South Carolina." DMin diss., Samford University Beeson Divinity School, 1998.

Stevens, R. Paul. *The Other Six Days: Vocation, Work, and Ministry in Biblical Perspective.* Grand Rapids, MI: William B. Eerdmans, 1999.

Stitzinger, James F. "Spiritual Gifts: Definitions and Kinds." *The Master's Seminary Journal* 2, no. 2 (2003): 143.

Wagner, C. Peter. *Your Spiritual Gifts Can Help Your Church Grow.* Ventura, CA: Regal Books, 2005.

Willimon, William. *Proclamation and Theology.* Nashville, TN: Abingdon Press, 2005.

Wimmer, Steven Dean. "Equipping the Saints for Service: A Systems Approach to Empowering Lay Ministry at Alma Church of God." DMin diss., Anderson University School of Theology, 2006.

Witherington, Ben, III. *Conflict and Community in Corinth: A Socio-Rhetorical Commentary on 1 and 2 Corinthians.* Grand Rapids, MI: William B. Eerdmans, 1995.

Wollensack, Peter. *Called to Be, Called to Do: Finding Your Purpose and Destiny in Your Unique Gifting.* Lima, Peru: Harvest Equippers, 2010.

Woodson, Carter G. *Mis-Education of the Negro.* Trenton, NJ: Africa World Press, 1933.